THE FIVE TYPES OF WOMEN TO AVOID IN THE HOOD

MCGREGOR PHILIPPE

THE FIVE TYPES OF WOMEN TO AVOID IN THE HOOD

iUniverse books may be ordered through booksellers or by contacting:

iUniverse
1663 Liberty Drive
Bloomington, IN 47403
www.iuniverse.com
1-800-Authors (1-800-288-4677)

ISBN: 978-1-5320-9281-7 (sc)
ISBN: 978-1-5320-9282-4 (e)

Library of Congress Control Number: 2020901749

Print information available on the last page.

iUniverse rev. date: 02/07/2020

CONTENTS

ACKNOWLEDGMENTS

Putting up this piece was not an easy task, but so many people helped smooth the path. This wouldn't have been possible without the prodigious aid I got from my adorable parents. You made discipline our culture, and it has helped me become a better person.

My sincere gratitude goes to Ariana Evans for her positive support. You have shown me that a conversation can make a difference. In a special way, I thank my brother Rick for his infallible words of wisdom. Those words were my support during the moments my strength failed me. I am eternally grateful to Queenzflip's *Blind Date* for assisting me in researching the different types of women.

To Juan Valdez of the Angryman Channel, who inspired me to write this book. I am ever grateful. Thank you helping me to show all the good men out there to avoid these types of women. I acknowledge Craig Hayes, one of the best attorneys in New York City involving domestic cases. You are amazing!

I would also like to thank Cheyanne Bruce, who inspired me to become better. You are a beautiful young teen with a bright future. I am so proud of you and would like your little sister to follow your path.

To every other person who has directly or indirectly contributed to this work: I acknowledge you all. No amount of words could sufficiently express the depth of my gratitude to you all.

My sincere thanks and gratitude goes to Almighty God, who made everything possible for the grace to make this project a reality. May his name be praised!

INTRODUCTION

Women are beautiful creatures, I admit, but there are different types. Some are more beautiful than others, and some are more deadly than others. My friend used to tell me that he had conducted research on the popular saying "Behind every successful man is a woman." He has discovered that behind a messed-up man is also a woman. Just as so many people have attained certain heights in their careers, financial independence, or love lives, because of a woman, so many people have lost properties, loved ones, and their lives because of women. A woman can make you, just like a woman can destroy you. For the purposes of this book, we are going to talk about not just any woman but women in the hood. When I say the hood, I mean the black community. Specifically, we are going to talk about the types of women in the hood you need to avoid.

The black community is filled with lots of chicks. I know this may be a new thing to you, especially if you are white or are not conversant with the activities of the hood. The occupants of the hood have distinct features that distinguish them from others. The chicks are of different types, and so are the dudes. There are the good ones, who possess all the good attributes you can think of. There are also bad eggs, those whom you pray to never meet again. I am tempted to say that these bad ones make up the greater population of the occupants of the hood. You may have encountered a few women who have affected your perception about the women from the neighborhood. You may have met a nice one, and you conclude that all of them are very nice. Or you may have received a cold attitude from one and so believe that they are all rude. This is not correct because every woman in the hood has her distinctive features.

I am going to discuss five types of women you should avoid in the neighborhood. This does not mean that they are the only women you will see in the hood, but they are the ones you should detect and avoid dealing with because the result can be disastrous. These women are everywhere in the hood. After reading this book, I am sure you will be able to point out these women, even if you have never taken note of them before now. Let us not forget that it is possible you will be among these women. The idea is to see how these acts affect the men and change them for the better.

Sometimes you see these guys who are perceived to be educated. They look enlightened and do not really fit in the hood, but they try to talk to some of the women in the neighborhood. These guys are oblivious to the kinds of women they are trying to talk to. If you talk to these women without knowing the things to watch out for, you'll miss the red flags telling you to flee, and then you are in for something big. You are liable to find yourself in deep shit at the end of the day. There are tons of things that can happen that are not good things when dealing with these kinds of women.

These sets of women I am outlining are toxic and corrosive. No matter how mean a man is, even if he is a thug, an armed robber, or an assassin, he can never be as mean as these women. They are worse than anybody, perpetuating the worst acts you can think of. It's advised that you get accustomed to their characteristics and watch out for them to avoid falling into the pit they dig for their victims. You could be talking to someone who can leave bullets in your body at will. You can be thrown behind bars or beaten seriously if you step on her toes and she decides to deal with you. You need to understand how they operate to know how to relate with them. They can go to any lengths to bring you down.

These women have varying degrees to which they can ruin your life.

- Minor degree
- Major degree

MINOR DEGREE

It is established that these sets of women will be involved in something that can lead to your downfall, but for a minor degree, they can decide to mess up your life a bit. They can hire some people to beat you up in the hood or publicly embarrass you. They may get some girls to throw things at you. Either way, they will only do things that will not bring serious harm to their victims. The victims get over it with time.

They usually use these acts of minor degree when you commit a forgivable offense to them or they want to show you how mean they can be. You may raise your voice at them, and they will show you the stuff they are made of.

A chick saw her boyfriend collecting a package from another girl. She went to him and asked why he would be talking to another girl in the hood. The guy wouldn't take the confrontation; he yelled at her while explaining that he was sent to help give the package to the person it was meant for, and he smiled at her because he was simply being nice. The chick didn't take it lightly with him. She called her friends together and planned how to embarrass the dude. They got raw eggs and threw them at him, laughing.

How these women feel about you also affects the degree at which they strike at you. Inasmuch as they are callous, these ladies are still human beings. Sometimes they love, even if they do not show it or want to accept it. They mess up your life a bit because they care for you and don't want to hurt you that much.

Kate was getting closer to Khali by the day. Although Khali had never asked her out, Kate adored and loved Khali. The relationship went on like this until Kate heard that Khali was dating another chick. She lacked the courage the ask Khali, but their friendship continued as normal. She was called one day to see things for herself. Upon seeing them, she flared up. With the help of her friends, she beat the chick beyond recognition, tore her clothes, and left marks on her body. Kate knew deep down that she still cared for Khali even though she was mad at him. The only thing she did to him was to give him a slap.

Kate could have done worse than that to Khali, but it was evident that her feelings for him betrayed her.

MAJOR DEGREE

These women can decide to deal with you by completely ruining your life. They may be talking to somebody you do not know about and will never approve of, or they have a baby daddy who is capable of perpetuating heights of evil and wouldn't hesitate to deal with you whenever she demands it. They can destroy your life beyond repair. You will not recognize yourself by the time they are done with you. When they set out to destroy you completely, they make your life seem useless, and you will see no reason to live. They can break any part of your body or hold you hostage. They can go to the extent of shooting you or any member of your family.

These women usually go to this extent when you commit hideous crimes against them. The crime can be emotional, physical, verbal, or social.

- **Emotional.** You hurt their feelings by lying to them or not doing those things you were supposed to do. You can also hurt them emotionally when you forget important events about them, such as their birthdays. They may get mad at you for declining their offers.

- **Physical.** You can offend them by using physical force on their bodies, such as pushing them, hitting them, or slapping them. These ladies get agitated once you offend them. They may find it hard to give you a second chance, and they'll deal with you for using physical force on them. These chicks can also take offense if they sense that you are going to beat them. They may want to attack first before you do whatever you plan to do to them. I saw a movie where a woman went to the next house to call out the other woman who lived there and said, "Hey, bitch, I know you have been thinking of fighting me. But you know what? I think the same way too. I am ready now, and I think we can get down to it." She started dragging the woman by her hair after completing her statement.

- **Social.** When you do anything in the neighborhood that would make them feel embarrassed, then you have offended them, and you are bound to face their wrath. Once they feel their immediate social group has an opinion about them that they are not comfortable with, and it's because of what you did or said, they will be ready to drink your blood. For example, if you have a one-night stand with a chick, and you come to the hood to tell every Dick and Harry about your escapade with her and how dirty she was, prepare for what is coming for you.

These types of women we discuss below can go to any lengths to make you feel how dissatisfied they are with you, even if it means taking your life.

Diana had been dating him for a while. Although they had been breaking up and making up, she had hoped that he would be her husband. One day, he opened up to Diana and told her that she was not the kind of woman he wanted to spend the rest of his life with. Diana did not banter with him. He was happy that he had crossed that bridge, and he invited Diana to his wedding.

On the wedding day, Diana came just like the other guests. She waited for the time they would exchange marital vows before she created a scene. She went to the altar and shot the couple. She gave that bride a shot in the leg, and she shot her ex-boyfriend in both legs and an arm. She told him that she would have killed him, but she needed him to stay alive so that both of them would suffer together.

Just like having tender feelings toward you can make these women deal with you on the minor level, they can deal with you seriously if they have harbored hatred for you before you offend them. If a chick does not like you, she can kill you if you mess with her sister or her friend. Let's say you have made comments about her that she has heard, but she kept quiet because you didn't talk to her directly. The very day you step on her toes, she will pay you back for everything at the same time.

CAUSES OF THE DIFFERENCES

So many things have contributed to forming these different types of black women. The causes are natural and beyond anyone's control, and they have stayed for a very long time so that they become the norm. They have formed the perceptions of these women, and they include social programming, cultural programming, and other situations.

- **Social Programming.** Social programming refers to those sets of instructions that we internalize as we grow up to fit into society. We subconsciously learn these instructions, and they become part of us. We are able to dictate what society frowns on because of social programming. One society may frown at an act, but another society accepts it. The family, one's peer group, and school are the primary agents of social programming. For example, some people believe that every child must follow a pattern of go to school, make good grades, graduate, get a good job, marry, and have children. A child who is born in this society will want to follow this pattern because it has been registered in his or her mind, though unknowingly. In another community, schooling is not necessary; a child can do anything he or she wishes to do, and there is no laid-down pattern.

These women who have stayed in the hood have unconsciously copied the practice of the hood. Some of them grew up in a kind of family where the mother was a baby mama who had many boyfriends across the hood. Others do not even have parents at all; the elder siblings go out to hustle for food. This doesn't mean that none of the occupants of the hood learned good habits. But a greater percentage—the ones I am talking about in this context—fully internalized the negative ones, and nobody frowns at it because it has become a norm.

- **Poverty Endured.** Hunger and poverty are the prevailing words in the black community. To an extent, hunger and poverty are hereditary in the hood. But all the occupants are not on the same scale of being poor. Some are poorer than others, meaning that some are in a more benign situation. Just the way the occupants are not equal in terms of wealth, the women are affected too. Most of the women have suffered and endured hatred for a long time. They get themselves involved in so many odd things just to make ends meet. Their experiences in the process of fending for themselves, which are usually ugly ones, shape their perception. Some develop a thick skin so they won't feel hurt anymore. Others feel so worthless that they can do anything not minding whether it dents their image.

- **Cultural Programming.** The cultural disposition of the occupants in the neighborhood affects them. Whereas some tend to work on themselves to boost their self-esteem, others develop low self-esteem, leading to the differences that are evident in these women.

- **Personal Experience.** Apart from the situations mentioned above, other things contribute to making the women in the hood different from one another, such as personal experience. This involves what the person has experienced in his or her immediate environment. A lady who was gang-raped as a child can grow up to crawl into her shell or become a nuisance in the community. This same lady would not be the same as a person who hasn't experienced rape. Despite the fact that mothers try to be mothers by training their children properly, their children are bound to drift their thinking toward their personal experiences in life.

I was talking with Cindy, a chick in our neighborhood. I asked her why she was cold on male folks, and she opened up that she'd seen how her father had treated her mother, as if she was an item without worth. Her mother died by her father's hands, and she swore to take revenge on any guy who crossed her path.

She has really kept to her promise, but as you can see, this act was born out of what she personally experienced.

TYPES OF WOMEN YOU SHOULD AVOID

Like I said earlier, there are many types of women, but our interest here is in those to avoid in the neighborhood. Better put, these women will cause you more problems than the others. In no particular order, these types of women are:

1. The thot
2. The mammy
3. The hood rat
4. The bad bitch
5. The educated ratchet

CHAPTER 1

THE THOT

You may be wondering what thot means. Thot is the short form for "that ho over there." Just like it sounds, it means that you can close your eyes, point to a corner, and say "that ho over there," and you will open your eyes to see that there is really a ho there.

This set of women is referred to as thots for two reasons. First, it's because of what the name stands for, meaning that they are very common in the hood. Second, it's because of their promiscuous nature. These thots make up the greater population of women in the neighborhood. If you are new to the hood, the first person you meet will probably be a thot. If you need to ask for directions from anyone in the hood, I am sure the person you see may be a thot. You can recognize them by sight.

FEATURES OF A THOT

The following are the prevailing features of thots in the neighborhood. If you are observant, it will take you seconds to ascertain these features.

They are very common in the hood.
They constitute the larger part

of the hood, and you may think they are just a normal kind of woman when you see them. Physically, you may easily spot them with their overt, too much, and funny makeup, but if you are new to the hood, you may overlook those signals. They do not exert superiority or look domineering. At first sight, you may want to be close to them.

Appearance. The thots are usually slim, or at least not too big. They look slender and doesn't gain weight quickly. Some people believe that their slim nature is because they don't eat well; others say they cannot add flesh because they are frustrated. Either way, it is quite unusual to see a fat thot.

Class. Thots are not ones whom you would consider classy. They are not fashionable. Sometimes they do not appear with makeup, but when they do, they look funny. Their makeup does the opposite of their intention. They may want to wear wigs to fit in, but wigs make them appear worse than they were without one. Some men can look at them and think they are not up to their standards; others may consider them to be homely. This appearance they put up is not because they do not want to look better; most times, it is because they do not have the means to buy those things. They cannot afford to buy the good weaves or the best makeup, but they want to use them. They manage the little money they have and are able to afford the cheap wigs, and they wear them that way.

The level they operate on is written all over them. They usually have cheap furniture, cheap animals, and plants around them. Their outfits also depict lowlifes. They are not stylish; they don't really have taste like that. They settle for anything they see.

They are usually promiscuous. They can fuck anybody and anywhere. They do not have a strong stance when it comes to giving their bodies to men. As a dude, you do not need to have much going on with them to get laid. You can start talking with them today and get them to fuck the same day as well. They have no shame. They do not practice the act of hiding somewhere to make love. They can have sex in the car, behind the car, in the backyard, or anywhere. They do not mind the person they are having sex with; they do not understand what it means for a man to have standards. Once they develop interest in you, they do not mind what you do, how much you earn, where you stay, or what you look like. A thot doesn't care using her body to pay for an item she buys.

They have low self-esteem. Thots attach no value to themselves. They think they are not worth anything. They hide in this cloak to easily frolic with anyone they see because they think they have no standards. They believe they have nothing to lose. A thot can sleep with so many men in the neighborhood that know each other, and she doesn't mind if one tells the others.

I was talking to someone the other day, and he told me that he discovered that a chick in the hood had been sleeping around with almost all his friends. She now lives with one of them but is not married to him. He loves her and went to confront her, trying to hold her to ransom by telling her that he would expose her. The chick did not even look bothered. She simply told him to go to hell and do anything he deemed fit; she didn't care.

The only thing I could tell the person was that she was a typical example of a thot.

These women never think highly of themselves. They believe whatever level they attain at a time is the best they can do. Within themselves, they believe that the men from the high end are not meant for them. They can only get for themselves those men who operate on a low standard.

The thots do not really understand parental love and care, especially coming from the father. Most of them do not even know their fathers. Some are the products of baby mamas, and others have lost their fathers. Some of them were rejected by their mothers at birth, leaving them with their fathers or alone to struggle for survival. The fact that they didn't grow up with a man in their lives means they know little about men. Maybe if they had experienced how fathers love and care for their children, especially their daughters; tell the bedtime stories; tuck them in bed at nights; protect them from harm; are ready to listen to them whenever they need someone to talk to; and support their children in their endeavors. Because they have no idea of how a man is supposed to treat a woman, they tend to take shit from any man. They believe that whatever they get is the way it is supposed to be.

CAUSES OF LOW SELF-ESTEEM AMONG THOTS

Thots are known for having low self-esteem. They have little or no confidence in themselves, which makes them not believe in themselves or trust their abilities. The following reasons contribute to how thots view themselves.

- **Lack of Parental Care**

Their lives as children and their transition into adulthood were not smooth. They lacked so many things, including experiencing real love from family and the people around them. It is normal to have people around you who can egg you on, tell you how strong you are, and encourage you to do better than you are doing, but the thots did not grow up in such an environment. They have no one to tell them and remind them of those beautiful parts of them. They didn't hear things like "You are really a strong woman," "I envy you," "You are beautiful," "I wish I could be like you," "You have beautiful eyes," or "I love you." They do not know that there is any good or truly beautiful thing about them. As a result of this, they grow into women who have low self-esteem.

- **Feeling Unloved; Negative Peers**

When children are not getting the necessary attention they deserve, it has an adverse effect on their personality. What we think of about ourselves is largely dependent on how others feel about us. If others see you in a bad view, you are obviously going to hate yourself. On the other hand, if other people perceive you to be a good person, you usually feel good about yourself. This is the same case with thots. They feel unloved because they do not get the warm feeling of acceptance in their environment.

In the same vein, being part of a social group where you feel you are not truly accepted can affect your view about yourself. These thots may have friends and belong to social groups that pressure them to do something they are not comfortable with and do not consider their thoughts or feelings. This makes thots think that they are good for nothing or that something is wrong with them. It therefore affects their perception of themselves. For example, a lady may want to wear a particular dress to a party, but her friends make her believe that her choice is the worst of all her choices, and they persuade her to wear another outfit. As little and flimsy as it sounds, repetition of acts like this can affect the person, making her feel as if she cannot make good choices herself.

- **Early Sexual Activity**

Their low self-esteem can also be caused by early involvement in sexual activity. Most of the thots became sexually active at a very early age. This makes them feel less of themselves, and they lose their self-confidence. They think they are worth nothing. This gets to a worse situation if the sexual act was one of force. If they didn't willingly give themselves to the man involved, they hate themselves even more. They think very low of themselves, believing that everyone else is better than them.

HOW TO IDENTIFY THOTS AS HAVING LOW SELF-ESTEEM

1. Negative thinking
2. Fewer expectations in life
3. Lack of self-confidence
4. Sadness and depression
5. Less ability to take compliments
6. Ignoring and neglecting their own needs
7. Lack of social skills

1. **Negative thinking.** Thots always think negatively about any situation. They do not think of the positive outcome for a situation. This is why they are scared of change. They believe that change will make things worse for them. They think that change will not favor them. They therefore choose to take things the way they see it.

2. **Fewer expectations from life.** Thots do not expect much from life. They do not have long-term goals. They are unsure about having greater things happen to them. They create a shell and hide inside it. They make this shell a comfortable place for themselves because they do not want to aspire for great things.

3. **Lack of self-confidence.** Thots have zero self-confidence. They grew up in a harsh environment where everyone was being critical and hostile to them. This leads to grown women who have no confidence, resulting in low self-esteem.

5. **Less ability to take compliments.** Because they weren't used to getting compliments as children, it becomes difficult to accept compliments. They even see the compliment as having a sarcastic undertone. They do not want to be told that they look good, and they do not see themselves as beautiful.

6. **Ignoring and neglecting their own needs.** These women ignore their needs because they do not see anything about them as worthy.

They see no need for attending to their needs; they would rather ignore them and concentrate more on their men's needs to keep them. A thot can have some amount of money she may want to buy clothes with, but she would rather spend the money on her boyfriend instead of using it to get some new clothes for herself.

7. **Lack of social skills.** These chicks do not get themselves involved in social gatherings. They settle with those few people whom they know and associate with instead of belonging to larger social groups. They feel intimidated in a large social gathering and therefore shy away from associating with large groups of new people. You may not see them at birthday parties, although from time to time, they may show their faces.

Attractiveness. Thots are not usually attractive. Most times, it's because they lack absolute confidence in themselves and choose to hide behind makeup and wigs to feel better about themselves. Their makeup looks ridiculous or funny because they didn't buy goodproducts, and they often do not apply the makeup appropriately. Their makeup looks rough, and their dressing is not pleasing. That notwithstanding, they know that they have a mask in the form of makeup and wigs, and therefore people will no longer see them for what they truly are (which they are not proud of), but for what they are comfortable showing. All these extra items are not just to appear attractive, but for them to have a better perception of themselves. The truth is that these things make them look worse.

Children. It is common for them to have at least one child out of wedlock. Almost every thot is a baby mama. But the way they go about sexual adventure, they often bear fruit. A thot can have five children from five different men.

When she bears these children, she makes attempts to raise the kids. She does not abandon them or leave them at the mercy of relatives. She hustles for her money and uses the money to provide for her children at the level she can afford.

Marriage. It is very difficult to find a thot who is married or in a long-term relationship. This does not mean that they do not get married or maintain a long-term relationship, but it is almost impossible to see one. You can see a married one, but the marriage is probably an arranged marriage, and one of the people will leave the other in a matter of time. You see them with titles like ex-girlfriend or ex-wife. This inability to stay with a man for a long time may be due to insecurity, lack of passion in the relationship, or seeing someone else whom they perceive to be better.

Breakups for thots don't necessarily need to have a cogent reason. They can wake up one morning and feel like they are no longer comfortable having you around, and before you know what is happening, they have called it quits and left with their belongings.

They have poor taste in style. Thots do not have good taste when it comes to fashion. They are not interested in what is in vogue or how to look their best. They are the worst set of people you can look up to or copy their outfits because that is not their major concern. Once they wear something and feel comfortable with it, they do not mind whether it is out of fashion. They lack the love people have to acquire new and trending things in order to appear good. Although some people say that their choice of clothing is relative to lack of resources, I think that these women wouldn't look much different if they were given enough money to shop. They simply don't see the need for dressing up in a fashionable manner. Their poor taste in style shows not only on their bodies but also in the other things they use, such as their furniture or their living space.

They have a fairly even temperament with other black women. They are easygoing and have a composed disposition with the other women in the hood. They are not hotheaded or hot-tempered when it comes to relating with their fellow women. It would be easier to believe that this set of women stage fights with their fellow women, but they actually relate well with them and do not exhibit unruly attitudes toward them. You need to get to a certain height before you can fault other people and insult them. You need to have a high opinion of yourself to be able to come out and openly challenge other people in the hood. They know of their social standing and are aware that the best way out of it is to be easygoing with the people around them, especially black women. Do not get me wrong: this does not mean that they do not have clashes with the other women, or they allow themselves to be the victims in any fight that involves other women in the hood. From time to time, they show the true stuff they are made of and deal with any woman who steps on their toes.

Intelligence. Most thots are not intelligent. If they were intelligent, they wouldn't be living like this. Only a few thots can think twice and make a better choice if the situation presents itself.

Thots are usually submissive. Thots stay in the hood, where they have been with so many guys in relationships. The guys they are dating do not mind snapping out at any time. To keep men, thots stomach everything the men do to them. Thots know when a boyfriend is going out with another woman, but they cannot say shit to the guy because he can use it as a reason for quitting the relationship, which the thots don't want. They can only meet or deal with the bitch with whom he is cheating on them.

In the process of keeping up with the shit they get from this guy, they learn to be good subordinators. These guys the thots are dealing with have already been to prison or may have just been released from prison, so they do not mind going back there. They may be doing something that will take them back to prison. These dudes do not give a shit about themselves, so there is absolutely nothing the thots can do to them, so they are submissive and accept their terms.

Employment. Most thots are sporadically employed. These women look for work aside from being promiscuous.

They can mess with anybody because of any or all of the following.

1. They have nothing to lose

2. They attach their self-worth to a third party
3. Orientation
4. They have multiple sex partners
5. They attach as a means of escape

1. **They have nothing to lose**. A thot is already known in the hood as being a promiscuous women. The occupants of the hood know what she does and the level she has gotten. She knows that she has no shame, and her reputation is one thing she is not interested in. She has nothing to lose by sleeping around with all the men in the neighborhood. Let's say the dudes start discussing her. The first dude may tell another about the thot's escapades. The reaction from the other dude will be something like, "That chick can't surprise me anymore. She has done worse things." The same thing happens when the second dude goes to tell another guy about her. For the guys she is messing with, they may hold their reputation in high regard, but the thots do not mind. Most times the guys run away from thots to save their names.

Jane is a thot who used to stay in my neighborhood. Her baby daddy, a good friend of mine, used to tell me things about her. One evening, we were sitting on the park bench in the hood to get some fresh air, and he started telling me about his baby mama. She had been going out with a married man in the hood and was caught red-handed in bed by the man's wife. It was a shameful scene. She couldn't wait for the flames of what she had committed to die down before she moved in with another man, who is said to be a very good friend of the married man. She had been living with him for weeks. It was not like I was surprised at hearing the story. As a matter of fact, I did not expect more from her.

While he was telling me the story, Jane came around and figured out that we were discussing her, and she said, "You all should go ahead and say the shit you wanna say about me. Just know that Jane doesn't care a dime about what you think of her."

In Jane's case, she was already aware of people's perception of her. She knew that whenever people talked about her, it was going to be something negative. This is the same with all thots.

2. **They attach their self-worth to the second party.** Another reason a thot will sleep around with guys in the hood and feel comfortable about it is if she attaches her worth to a man. Just like I said earlier, a thot lacks confidence in herself and has low self-esteem. To boost this self-esteem, she sees the guys as her host and feeds on the guy's worth. She wants to identify with the person's personality because she cannot build her own. She assumes that what the guy has attained is hers as well.

Ella has seen herself as someone who cannot be better than she is already. She derives pleasure in jumping from one guy's car to another in the hood. Maybe a bed would have been better, but she is always seen having sex in the cars. A new dude just moved in. To an extent, the dude was doing well for himself. Ella wasted no time in identifying with this guy, and shortly afterward, she moved in with him. Now, she goes around bragging with the guy's achievements.

Ella has forgotten that they are two different people. She sees what the dude has attained as her success as well.

3. **Orientation.** It cannot be denied that the orientation these chicks got while growing up led to their multiple sex partners. They have grown up in a household where the mother was a thot. A thot grew up knowing her mama's boyfriends and seeing them come to the house to sleep with her. Invariably, it registered in her subconscious that this act must be a good one. Her mother may not be the only one. Her neighbors may also be doing the same thing. The girl would feel comfortable about that idea from childhood and grow into it.

Once, I heard some thots talking among themselves. I couldn't help listening to their discussion. They were talking about how they'd grown up and how they saw their mothers or guardians. The bottom line of the stories was their mothers had so many men and didn't give a fuck what people said. One confirmed that her mother left her in the house and went to live with her latest boyfriend.

These women cannot grow into better women. We tend to copy our role models, and the mothers served as the role models. Because their mothers were promiscuous, then it isn't a shock if they turn out to be promiscuous too.

4. **Multiple sex partners.** Thots have had a lot of sexual activity with different men. These different men have opened thots' eyes to the divergent ways of getting pleasures through sex. The thots wants to experiment more to satisfy their desire. A typical thot has lost count of how many men she has slept with. She may be counting by a fraction, such as, "What fraction of the men in the hood have fucked you?"

I met a thot at a party and started talking with her. I don't know whether she said these things because she had taken a reasonable quantity of alcohol. She told me that she enjoys sex too much, beyond her own comprehension. She sees herself getting close to men who enjoy sex too. Even if they have no strings, she simply wants to go down on them. The more she sleeps with men, the more she wants more men. She said that it has gotten to the extent that when she goes out with her friends on weekends, they may end up sharing the same dude in the same session. According to her, she used to be ashamed of how many men she slept with, but not anymore. She has taken it as her lifestyle, as something that is natural.

I have observed that the more thots sleep with men, the more they want men, and I concluded that sleeping with men increases their sex drive.

5. **As a means of escape**. It is obvious that the thots do not live self-fulfilling lives. They get negative tags from people (prostitute, lowlife, and so on), which is not the kind of life anyone wants to live. They are not satisfied with their lives. They think they have no goals or achievements.

One of the things that gives them joy about their existence is sex. They leverage sex to make themselves happy.

I listened to an interview that was granted by one chick in my neighborhood whom I consider to be a thot. She openly admitted that whenever she gets mad at herself or feels like she is disappointed in herself, it takes good sex to get her back to normal.

The thots are aware that the harsh realities of life are directly facing them, and they therefore carve a place they can run to for succor, which is sex.

Thots may not be a perfect symbol of motherhood, but they work really hard to take care of their children. It depends on how many kids they have; if they have a couple of children, they may get government welfare, but most times they get jobs. They may get a job at the lower end of the medical line or customer service. If they get calls for a job, just know that there are a lot of thots applying. You see them working as libarians, nontutorial staff, and so on.

They have a low level of entitlement. They retain some of their traditional habits such as cooking and cleaning. It is quite an amazing part of them, though it is difficult to believe that they cook and clean. I have conducted research on them, and I found out that they cook and clean at home. They cook for their children or boyfriends. If they meet a new dude, it won't take much time for them to go live with the guy and cook and clean. If they start talking to a guy, they wouldn't mind going to cook and clean for him. The same thing happens if they have a one-night stand with a guy in his house. They wake up the next morning and clean and cook for the guy. I know lots of ladies who are thots, but they do a lot of cleaning and cooking at home. In doing these chores, they unconsciously teach their children how to do them. The children grow up to do the chores too. They also use the money they make to bring home needed materials.

Thots can be submissive to a man. They can cook and clean, and they make attempts to raise their children by providing for them.

They are hustlers. They can do anything that puts money in their pockets, whether legal or illegal. You can see them in all sectors that involve money transactions. They hustle their asses to make money.

- **Legal business.** They can do anything that has the government backing to make money. Their aim is to go home with some dough at the end of the day. They can work as assistants in every sector, and they can buy and sell items. Thots are the people one would call real hustlers. They fight tooth and nail to make ends meet. If you see any lady in the hood who is able to find and keep their jobs, that chick is likely to be a thot.

- **Illegal business.** Just the way thots venture in legal businesses to make money, they do not mind doing illegal things to cater to their needs. Their objective is to make sure that money comes in; they do not care the means. They can sell weed or cocaine, and they even do human trafficking (but that is at the extreme end). They can do all sorts of shit to get paper.

Marriage. They do not marry. This is not because they do not want to marry. Some factors come together to hamper their being successfully married.

1. Their inability to sustain a relationship
2. The kind of guys they roll with

1. **Their inability to sustain relationship.** Thots do not last in their relationships. There is always one reason or another that they break up. It can be a prolonged endurance, where the guy is constantly beating or mistreating them. It can be that they are constantly cheating on the guy, and he finds out. Whatever the reason, they find it difficult to stay with one man for a long time.

Once, a chick came complaining that she didn't know what was wrong with her. She was beginning to doubt that she was normal. She had tried to stay in relationships with guys, but there had always been reasons to break up. The first guy complained he was always seeing her around guys. The second guy left her because she wouldn't concede to aborting her baby. He didn't want the baby, but she did. It caused a fight, and the guy left. The third guy was a Casanova, and he flirted with any female. The annoying part was that he did it in front of her. The fourth guy wanted her to give him all the proceeds from her sales, and she told him how impossible it was. It led to daily fights and eventually a breakup.

I was tempted to tell her that she was a thot. She needed to do more work on herself to have a different and better experience.

2. **The kind of guys they meet.** These women usually get into relationships with guys who do not value marriage. These guys either do not have interest in marriage or are not ready to provide for a family. What they do is to talk thots into having the same ideals as them. It is very easy for them to achieve this because they have played their roles well in the lives of these thots. The guys can tell them, "We don't need a ring to be together. We are okay the way we are. We are here for each other; it is needless to do another form of consolidation." The guys know that they are not being honest with their assertions, and they back it up with actions. They give the chicks love, attention, or money (if they can afford it) to calm nerves. They do anything for the chicks to make them feel comfortable without even talking about marriage. They use the people around them to give the thots examples of where relationships failed even after marriage, or succeeded without marriage. This makes the ladies forget about marriage, and most times they stay with these guys to bear them children or be companions.

I have a friend who said to me, "Mike, I ain't gonna marry a woman with my hard-earned money. All she would bring me is nothing but stress. I would rather get a woman to live with so that if she messes up, I can show her the way out of my house." He has a chick in the hood and made her believe that he was a guy with lots of prospects. Whenever the chick talked about marriage, he would tell her that they did not need marriage. They were okay as they were, and marriage may change what they felt for each other. This scene replayed at times, and my dude did not think of what to say to her anymore. He opened his mouth, and words started rushing out. Now, the chick has gotten accustomed to it. She does not talk about marriage anymore.

The way people act depends on the thoughts they have nursed over time. People can change other people's ideas, actions, or activities by changing the way they view those things. This is exactly what happens to the thots: they forget about marriage entirely or change their perception of marriage.

Traditional type. By traditional type, I mean what a thot would be if not for social and cultural programming. In the absence of all this programming, a thot would be "a ride or die" chick. This is the type of chick who does not mind living with a man for her whole life without getting married to him. You remember those women your uncles never married? They had bitches who were with them for a while. That type of chick is a "ride or die" chick. They roll with the guys for a long time, not minding the direction the relationship going.

My uncle had one. I used to complain about it, but the chick came to confront me to stop fighting her. She was proud to tell me that she had stayed with my uncle for twelve years, and she was going nowhere. She said she was ready to stay with my uncle for as long as she breathed. I suggested she get my uncle to marry her, and she told me that marriage was overrated. She was fine with my uncle the way they were, and she was not aiming for a level as high as marriage. In fact, the attention my uncle gave her was better than nothing.

After hearing from her, I realized that separating her from my uncle was not something anyone could just do. She has made her decisions and would stand by him for life. The fact that would baffle you is that she never cheats on him. She stands by him at all times.

Ratchet level. The thots can be nasty. They can be crazy, but most times you do not know how crazy they are until you have an encounter with them. They are the women who will tear your clothes if you try to fight with them.

Remember that this woman has no shame and has attached no value to herself. You do not want be involved in any fight with her. This is a chick who will say any nasty thing about you or body shame you. If she makes attempts to talk to you, and you give her attitude, she may say things like, "I wonder why he is acting as if he came from heaven? Does your mama have a better look?"

They are traditional. They can be traditional to an extent because:

1. They can adjust and be in a long-term relationship
2. They can be submissive to the right kind of dude
3. They make attempts to raise their children

1. **They can adjust and be in long-term relationships.** When they meet someone they have genuine feelings for, they can be in that relationship for a long time, not minding the outcome. The guys they are in this relationship with may not think of marrying them, but they are okay with it. They can cheat on their boyfriends and make up with them, but in most cases they remain faithful.

2. **They can be submissive to the right kind of dude.** They find themselves in an environment where everyone knows them, and if they are not careful, they may lose their boyfriends. For peace to reign, they maintain a calm nature and endure whatever is coming from the dude because they can do little to nothing to salvage the situation.

3. **They make attempts to raise their children**. They try as much as they can to provide for their children. They look after their children by

seeing to their welfare. They also cook for them, clean the house, and teach them how to do the same.

IMPLICATIONS OF DEALING WITH A THOT

It is very possible that the first chick you meet in the hood is a thot. You may have talked to one before now without knowing it. They are so common that you have an 80 percent chance of talking with a thot if you visit the hood. That is how common the thot is.

This is the kind of chick whom you see on those videos that are leaked online, where a guy is fucking a chick in the garage. That's her! She has no shame and can do anything with any man. You may ask, "What would a dude be doing with a chick who has no value for herself?"

Dealing with this woman would leave you at the level you were financially when you met her, or worse. She won't allow growth or anything that looks like it. If you were making five hundred a day when you met her, you will likely make that amount or less every day of your life until you leave her. If you were staying in the slum with her, you will remain in that slum as long as you are with her. No growth! No improvement! This is what the thot reduces you to.

These chicks cannot maintain a long-term relationship. They jump from one dick to the other. They can never be satisfied with one man's dick. She is traditional, but being traditional alone does not make a whole woman. If you think you are going to stay with this woman and change her into a better person, you have another thing coming because this chick does not want to be better than she is. She is very satisfied with her kind of lifestyle.

This chick is a dream killer. You cannot give yourself a target and hang around this chick. The moment you try to get better, earn more, or go for an upgrade, you will experience a push back from her. You can achieve nothing with this woman by your side. You need to run away from her.

WHY SHOULD YOU AVOID THE THOTS

Now that I have created a mental picture of the thot, I can tell you why you must avoid thots. It is worthy to note that of all the types of women you should avoid, the thots are the ones who cause the least problems. Compared to other types of women in the hood, the problems that come with associating with a thot are minor.

The following are reasons why you should avoid dealing with a thot.

1. **They are not very ambitious.** They do not strongly desire anything—a position, wealth, or a title. They are comfortable where they are. If they have one outfit to their name, they are very comfortable with it and do not want to grow. They settle for the less and accept what comes their way. They can get stuck in their way, and they will relax, not thinking about how best to move on. They do not aspire to be better than they are. They are not ready to go the extra mile to get things done.

While growing up, I knew Julie, a young woman who sells provisions in the hood. At that time, she was the only one selling such wares in the neighborhood, so everyone was her customer. She sold a great deal, and I used to go there to sit or play with my friends. Now I am grown, and Julie still sells this same provisions, almost the same scale. Nothing has changed except the barricade on the shop, which is looking a bit worn. She didn't grow the business despite the fact that she had lots of people patronizing her. She remained at the same level. I asked around and observed her, and I discovered who she was. She settles for what is available and not what is obtainable. The behavior has affected her boyfriend, though he won't accept it. He runs a garage situated in a very good site, yet nothing seems to change about the garage or about him year in and year out.

This couple can do better than they are doing already, but the fact that the woman is operating without ambition or goals affects whatever they are doing. If the chick had done better, it would be overtly seen in what the dude does as his business.

This behavior is contagious. People say, "Tell me your friend, and I will tell you who you are." If your friend has ambition, you are likely to be very ambitious. If it's the other end of the spectrum, you will be affected too. It may sound nice that they are satisfied with what they have. You as the guy would be the real king, giving orders while she obeys. Although you cannot run away from all arguments and disagreements, you may have done so from time to time. But you would be at the helm of affairs; she would never have a thought of dominating you. She would never think of overruling you or going against your orders. Whatever you say stands, especially if you are a thug. Thots totally submit to thug niggas. If you're a thug, she will never try to outsmart you because you know exactly what she is about. That notwithstanding, she will pull you down without you knowing it.

The thot has no goals or dreams. We used to write essays in school called "What I want to be when I grow up." This is not what you want this kind of woman to write because she obviously thinks nothing about the future. The only thing that comes to her mind is the moment. She helps herself with sex, money, and taking care of her children. This shit is like a communicable disease. Even in your circle, if you roll with people who are complacent, you will discover that with time, you will start behaving and thinking like them. The same thing happens if you are dealing with a woman who is complacent: you are bound to learn the habit too. She will transfer the disease to you, and you won't even notice it.

2. **They are not willing to embrace change.** They take the situation the way it is and do not want anything to change. It does not matter to them whether it is changing for better or worse. They find it hard to elevate their current situation to the next level. If they get employed as

a CNA, they will never think of improving themselves and becoming better than a CNA. They are ready to work at that same level for ten years, and they never think of becoming a nurse or something higher in the medical field.

A chick who lives with her man was always seen fighting with her boyfriend. Whenever they fought, you would hear her say so many things. If you listened to her, you would discover that she would be insulting the dude because of his new job. She would say things like, "You are looking like a big monkey in those cheap clothes you are wearing." She would complain that the guy left her at home every morning and came back late at night. Her boyfriend had changed, as she puts it. He didn't care about her anymore, and he didn't give her a good morning kiss anymore because he was always in a hurry to leave for work. She didn't care if he made a lot of money—she wanted her old boyfriend, not the new one. This drama ensued every day, and at a point the dude had to quit his job to get peace of mind.

This chick was aware that if the guy got paid in this job for a while, their financial status could be elevated, but she was scared of change. She had settled for what she was seeing. She didn't want a situation where things would change.

If you are around this kind of chick, you will be at the same level you have been for a very long time because she will pull you down. This is like guilt by association. These women are complacent, and they also transfer the complacency to you. You will find it difficult to work hard and attain more height. If you try, the moment you start getting more and making more out of life, you will experience serious pushback from her. She will start coming up with things that discourage you. If you get a good-paying job in a cooperate establishment, she may remind you of how miserable you look when you dress in a suit and tie. She will tell you that you are acting different and remind you how you used to be before you changed. If you try to move out of the hood or do anything differently, she won't welcome the idea. She wants you to remain as you are because she cannot stand upgrading. I call them enemies of progress because they are tying themselves down, and you as well.

WHY DO THOTS RESIST CHANGE?

The following are possible reasons thots do not want themselves or their partners to change. Human beings are unpredictable, and they can change for the better or for the worse. Thots see change of any kind as something that has negative consequences to the relationship.

1. **Loss of control.** They believe they will lose the connection they have with their guys. This feeling of insecurity makes them resist any form of change because a change will expose their guys with to many people and opportunities, and the men will be bound to lose interest in what they used to share with the thots. In order to avoid this, thots tend to hold on to what they have and relish in it, not minding how big or how small it is.

2. **Uncertainty:** Thots are uncertain of what tomorrow may bring in their relationship. They do not want to aim high or aspire to be greater than they are already. They prefer to remain mired in misery than to venture into the unknown. They believe the devil you know is better than the devil you don't. They prefer to manage their lives with their boyfriends rather than let the guys grow more, because thots can't be sure of the outcome.

3. **They are not prepared to bear the consequences of change**. They are aware that change has implications. They do not want a situation that demands a lot from them in terms of decision making and more responsibilities.

4. **They do not want a different atmosphere.** Change is meant to bring something different. A thot is not interested in how different things are going to be. She would rather savor what she is able to get at

this particular point in time. Too many differences may be confusing, and thots are not ready for that.

5. **Concern about competence**. A thot knows that a change in status can bring a change in likes and tastes. She doesn't know whether she can handle such a situation. If the guy starts earning more, he will want to eat food with a better taste, and she is not sure she can provide those things the way he wants them. Also, a change in status can lead to a totally new way of being, meaning that she has to start learning him all over again. A thot does not want to take chances.

CHAPTER 2

THE MAMMY

The mammy is another type of women you should avoid. They are also a very common archetype in the hood, like the thots. It is arguable which is more common. If you enter the hood ten times, you will see a mammy ten times. You may be wondering what I mean by mammy. I am sure you have seen tons of mammies before now. I am going to give you a perfect description of the mammy.

FEATURES OF THE MAMMY

Appearance. She looks overweight. You may see a mammy, a woman of thirty, and she will look fifty. Some of them have the right curves at the right places despite being overweight, but others are shapeless. They use funny makeup and weaves as well. They wear clothes that are overtly inappropriate for big women. In the looks department, the mammy looks like the thot, but the only difference is that she looks obese. They move around the hood as if nothing is wrong with being obese. As a matter of fact, they are actually proud of their body size. You cannot body shame them because they have convinced themselves that being big is normal. If you try to talk to them about weight-related issues, they insult you, and you go home thinking that you are the one who is not normal.

They are those large women in the neighborhood who wear too tight clothes that show the parts that are supposed to be hidden. You see them walking around the hood as if the world revolves around them. They do not care what they look like as long as they are comfortable in the outfit and feel beautiful. They are those women whom you need to remind that they are large. Their makeup speaks volumes. You must notice their makeup once you look at them. I am not sure whether they know how ugly the makeup makes them look. The same applies to the weaves in their hair. They only get something they are okay with and do not seek to please the public.

I am sure you have seen this type of woman. They are the BBWs, the big and sexy, and the "I don't fuck with the skinny" bitches. These women are big and bold. These chicks are not really described as fat. They are big-boned, and they have thick skin. They are similar to thots in so many ways. Mammies are not classy or fashionable, just like the thots. They get those items they need like clothes, weaves and more, but at an average level or below. They get the ones they can afford. They are not classy, and they go for cheaper articles despite the fact that they can afford more expensive ones. Mammies are usually not good looking. Because they are not good looking, they think they need to do more makeup up because they are not proud of their looks. They feel the need to get some weaves, and they use these items to engage their look, but it makes them look worse. Those things they do to enhance their look turn out to do the opposite.

The mammy is that chick in the hood with weird makeup and a weird hairdo—purple lipstick, funny-looking eyebrows, too much powder and blush, shiny red lipstick, and ridiculous colorful weaves.

Normally when a woman is big, she will avoid dressing in a certain way so that she won't draw attention to herself. These women wear nude colors, dress smart, and don't dress in a manner that would make them stand out and be easily noticed. They downplay the parts of them that they are not proud of, and they end up looking classy.

The following are ways in which fat women dress to look classy.

Fat women wear certain clothes to highlight some of their features, and some clothes hide parts they do not want people to notice. They understand that being overweight doesn't mean that they cannot look great. It takes a little know-how and a dose of confidence.

1. **They build a strong wardrobe**. In getting their clothes, they consider the shape of the cloths, the color, the pattern, and more. The color and pattern of clothes you wear can draw people's attention or distract them from areas on their bodies. Dark colors hide those portions, whereas bright colors highlight them. They can use bright colors in the places they want to accentuate, and they use dull colors in those areas they want to hide. For example, they can wear a light-colored belt over a darker shirt if they want to draw attention to their waistline. Clothes with big patterns make someone look bigger, whereas clothes with smaller patterns make one look smaller. They therefore go for outfits with smaller patterns to enhance their looks.

Clothes with horizontal stripes make one look bigger. They exercise caution with clothes that are striped horizontally. If you want to look bigger in the bust area, you can wear a blouse with horizontal stripes; it will draw attention to the bust, and the stripes will enhance the bustline.

For areas they want to highlight, they avoid ruffles. Ruffles can be attractive. People's attention will easily be drawn to ruffles. It can only be worn in those parts you want to emphasize. However, it can overemphasize a woman who is large chested. For the parts you would want a smaller look for, wear gathered fabric. Do not forget to try on the outfit. Go for clothes with colors that look great on you. A flattering color can complement your skin tone, whereas the wrong color will make you look washed out.

2. **They wear well-fitting undergarments.** They wear undergarments that are very supportive because they know that underwear is the foundation of the look. It is difficult to look great when the underwear is not supportive enough. They wear good bras not just because it helps them look good but because it helps avoid backache. To lose a bit of girth around your hips and thighs, wear low-legged, high-waisted underwear in a firm, supportive cotton.

Make sure the undergarments cover the areas they are supposed to cover. Pants that are too tight can reveal the linings on your outfit.

They go for tailored skirts and trousers and avoid flare skirts and wide-leg trousers. Shapeless clothes like one-size dresses and broomstick skirts are not for big people. Something that has a nipped waist goes better.

If you are looking for a skirt, an A-line cut is always a perfect fitting. Pencil skirts are not proper for fat people because it shapes and outlines the hips and waist. Skater skirts are a good piece for everyone.

Skinny or straight leggings in a dark wash fits every individual. They go for it. Leggings have a different fitting for everyone. If it is worn with a long shirt or dress, it gives a slimming or fashionable look, but if the person has a large bottom, thighs, or hips, it may look horrible.

They use middle-rinse jeans to flatter their shape. Alison Deyette, a stylist and fashion director, says, "Look for mid-rise styles to help flatten the tummy. It will act as a simple shaper. Avoid low rise! Your tummy will only pop out or hang over the lower waistline of the pants."

3. **They dress to flatter the top half.** This can be easy or difficult depending on body type.

Fat women should go for a shaped T-shirt instead of a straight T-shirt and untailored dresses. These shaped shirts are fitted closely to their natural waist and shoulders. They avoid spaghetti traps. They know that their bra straps might be wide, so they wear shirts that cover the bra straps. They do not go for blouses or jackets with cropped lengths. Full-length blouses fit better.

They wear skinny jeans or leggings with a tunic-style top that is not flowing. Wearing a top like that, not well fitted, will go well with the skinny jeans because the bottom half looks well tailored.

4. **Accessories that match**. Beautiful accessories not only make your wardrobe more versatile but also are blind to weight gain or loss. Tiny earrings and pendants may disappear on a big person, whereas large jewelry can overwhelm the audience. Also, a big handbag makes them look smaller because it doesn't look tiny next to them. A good number of bangles—say, three to four of them—can help make big women's plump wrists look slender. They wear long dangling earrings because they elongate the neck.

A good pair of shoes makes wearing a skirt or pants a positive joy. They do not go for delicate or flimsy footwear because they have heavy legs and angles. Wearing such footwear makes them look as if they are about to fall over or sink into the floor. On the other hand, a wedge is their perfect fit.

5. **Makeup.** When it comes to makeup, fat ladies prefer wearing nudes that highlight their natural face. Colorful makeup would make them look like comic relief. The hairdo should be simple and natural, not complex colors and ridiculous styles.

These women, though fat, dress better, but it is not the same with the mammy. Mammies do not have an excuse that they do not have enough money, yet they look shabbily dressed. Inasmuch as a mammy looks likes a thot except for the size, unlike the thots, mammies overvalue themselves. Remember that thots undervalue themselves, they find themselves in an environment where white is the standard of beauty, and they grow up having self-esteem issues. But with mammies, the opposite is the case. The big girls do not rely on beauty alone because being big is not the US standard of beauty. They have a stronger personality than the thots, and they use their personality to compensate for their big size. They have embraced the fact that they are big, and the best thing they can do for themselves is love themselves the way they are.

Attitude. Before now, ladies who are of a big nature try to beautify themselves with good behavior and a good attitude because they know that they are at a disadvantage. You hear men say things like, "Big woman are the best because they often have good characters." They look for big women when it comes to marriage.

I had a friend who told me that if he didn't meet a big lady, he wouldn't marry, and he maintained it. I got interested in the idea and went to make inquiries. Upon further enquiry, I discovered that was true to what he said, the plump ladies had good hearts and were better in taking a wife role than their skinny counterparts. I saw some of them myself and heard stories of what people experienced. But now the story has changed. They have become the opposite of what they used to be. I doubt my friend would maintain that same stance today.

There is a mammy in my hood. Whenever she passes, she feels people are looking at her and forming opinions about her, especially when she comes across a group of people sitting and discussing things. She feels they are talking about her. To show that she knows what they are saying about her, she formed a habit of talking out loud whenever she sees a cluster of people. She starts saying, "I don't owe nobody, any fucking person can talk shit about me." She voices it to everyone. The last time, her eyes caught a guy staring at her, and she approached the guy and confronted him. She warned him on a serious note to never again look at her in that manner.

Nowadays, our culture has changed so much that mammies do not think that they need to have a good attitude or anything else. They view themselves in a certain way. They see themselves as if they are better than any other chick on this planet. This is where their nasty behavior is rooted. This is where wearing loud clothes, colorful weaves, and makeup comes from. It is normal that once a person feels like she has attained a certain level, she is bound to start misbehaving, and that is the case with the mammy. Mammies believe they are gods and therefore are good all round. They suffer this delusion because they can attract as many men as the thot, however they do not realize that this is due to black men's self-esteem.

WHY DO MAMMIES HAVE OVERINFLATED SELF-ESTEEM?

One of the reasons that these big chicks have overinflated ego is that they can get as many men as they want. Mammies know that they have big and accentuated bodies that draw men of different walks of life. They leverage that fact, and it makes them develop confidence in themselves. It wouldn't take them time to walk down the street before they have started talking to another guy. Getting guys around them is like getting water to drink, and they know this.

A mammy is someone who will tell you not to worry about her boyfriend; if he messes up and leaves, she will get another one. In fact, before he leaves, she has three other guys on standby. Her ego is second to none. Her ability to draw as many men as she wants adds to her self-worth.

She can wear clothing that is obviously not appropriate for her and head straight to the club. There and then, she will get guys coming over to tell her how beautiful she is. A mammy thinks this is possible because of her beauty, her unbeatable attitude, or her incomparable charisma. The mammy believes that everything is all about her and that she can carry herself high. Mammies think that they are the only women who exist, and every other person can go to hell.

Some days ago, I saw one at the club. She was wearing an outfit that looked like sleeping clothes—it was way bigger than her, and the color looked all flushed out. I wondered why someone thought of dressing this way at a club. While the thought was still running through my mind, a guy came over to talk to her, paid for her drinks, and engaged her in a conversation. Shortly afterward, I saw her talking to another guy. In a short time, I saw her dancing with yet another guy. I was shocked. It didn't end there. She went home with a fourth guy.

They can easily attract these men because of the black men's low self-esteem and willingness to settle with certain types of women. This is because the black man is at the bottom when it has to do with resources. It is believed that with money, one can get for himself any woman he desires. It's not just because women love money, but they also want comfort. Money can help someone be comfortable in life. These other types of men have the resources and can get for themselves any kind of woman they want. They do not consider dealing with a woman who is overweight. Black men do not have that option. They settle for the one who is available. Also, some black men actually like bigger chicks. As they put it, they like them big chicks with big assets.

Out of curiosity, I have gone around the hood asking dudes why they are dating or marrying women I call mammies. I got different responses. "I love her." "She knows my needs and attends to them." "She is a good cook and keeps the house clean." "I love her size." But then they mention one particular thing that's worthy of note. No matter how they frame the reason, they always end with, "She is the kind of woman I can take care of." They feel those women's needs are not beyond their means and the resources they can provide. This is one of the reasons the guys can consider taking them as wives.

HOW TO HANDLE THE MAMMY'S SELF-IMPOSED EGO

1. Connect with your own inner security. Finding your own inner sense of security is the best way to handle mammies. Find your own confidence and stand by it. Then you can face these mammies without getting intimidated by the way they carry themselves. Once you feel secure, you can withstand these big ladies regardless of the kind of stones they throw at you.

2. Find their inner being and communicate with it. This is a simple step that's not simple to achieve. Learn how to ignore the annoying attitude that comes from these big ladies. Find out those attributes that are worth knowing or exploring. There is nobody who is entirely bad. No matter how ugly a person is, there must be something nice about that person. You may see a nice person who is clothed with a nasty attitude underlying this big woman. Find out ways you can enjoy each other's company. It would be an advantage to both of you.

3. **Know their secret.** Normally, people who overvalue themselves are quite insecure within. They tend to cover their feelings of insecurity by dominating and controlling others, and they find it difficult to accept that they are wrong. Mammies belong to this circle. When you are aware that they are running from their reality, you can know how to deal with them when they attack. You know what to say to them when they pick up a fight.

4. **Learn how to tolerate.** To stay with these big ladies, your tolerance level must be 100 percent. Do not be quick to judge them. Learn how to use patience to subdue situations, especially when your reaction would fuel the tension. If you are dating or marrying these large women, you must master the act of tolerance. Understand what motivates her, and think about how you would tackle the situation.

5. **Improve your assertiveness.** Mammies are very smart and can smell self-doubt miles away. When they do, they are likely to feed on it to deal

with their prey. The best way to handle this is to work on your own assertiveness. Mammies, with their bossy attitudes, won't try messing with someone they can't easily push around.

6. **Be tactful.** After you have worked on your assertiveness and improved it, you have a new weapon to engage: tact. Deal with them in a sensible manner. They should not be able to predict your actions. Wait, make calculations, and then strike if there is need for it. Sometimes you may choose to follow them with empathy and kindness.

7. **Change the subject of the conversation**. Another efficient tool you can use to clip the wings of the mammies is changing the topic of discussion. If she is trying to exert dominance by making it clear that she makes a lot of money working her ass out, change the topic to a TV series that both of you have watched. It will clear the tension.

Children. Most mammies have two or more kids out of wedlock. They are excited about having children because there is this belief that it will be difficult for a big woman to bear children. When they successfully deliver, they are very happy about it. They happily show off their kids from time to time. When they go out with them, they may call out their names often, sometimes for no reason, just to show the people around that the children belong to them. Mammies are those mothers who attend birthday parties with their children, and throughout the parties, you hear them scream, "Junior, come this way! Junior, I don't want to see you near that pool."

They are happy to introduce their children to you whenever you go on a visit, not minding whether they have made the introduction before.

Marriage. Mammies, unlike thots, have the potential to stay in a long-term relationship or eventually get married. This may sound impossible, but there is a specific reason. I refer to it as the big mama effect. We all grew up with a big mama in the house. Big Mama wasn't big her whole life. She got big after she gave birth and got older. If you check her pictures when she was younger, you will see that she was slender and very pretty. She got bigger as she got older. Psychologically for black men, these mammies remind them of their own big mamas. It brings those welcoming feelings of Big Mama and the comfort she brings. She would wash for you, clean for you, be on the lookout for you, give you money, and make things easily accessible for you.

I had a big mama. In those days, she would shout my name in the house for one reason or the other. Either she had something for me, or I had committed one crime or another. Inasmuch as I didn't like the way she used to pitch my name every time, I loved her so much. She did most of the things that were supposed to be my job. She did the dishes, cleaned up the house, did the washing, and cooked for me. On most occasions, after cooking she would come over to my room to call me to eat. Whenever she stepped out of the house, I was sure she would come back home with something for me no matter how small it was. She has a special place in my heart.

This image is what the black man sees in the mammies. Just the way I hold my Big Mama in a special way, other black men have special places in their hearts for their big mamas. Unconsciously, the black man doesn't have issues with a big woman because of this big mama image. The way he related to his big mama would make it easy for him to settle with the mammy without considering her size. He believes he would likely get the same things from this Mammy that he got from his big mama.

I know of a certain young man. He came to our hood to look for one of the mammies. She would insult the hell out of him and give him tons of reasons why she can't be with him. The young man never gave up. He kept coming despite the insults they rained on him. One day after the mammy gave him the day's dosage of insult, I went over to him and asked him why are you taking these insults. He told me that this woman was a complete replica of his grandma. He used to be very close to his grandma before she passed, and now what he saw in this woman was exactly what he saw in his granny. The worst part was that he didn't see anything wrong with her insults. He saw it as the normal nagging coming from his granny. He said he was ready to marry this woman there and then, if only she accepted him in her life. I heard he later married the lady, and the marriage turned out well.

This is the real reason black men do not mind marrying or settling down with the mammy, irrespective of her size: because she reminds them of their big mamas.

Ratchet Level. Mammies are known for their nasty attitude and are believed to have a high ratchet level. Mammies have more attitude than thots. Just as discussed earlier, back in the days, big women were known to be nice because of their pleasant attitude and endearing qualities. This behavior they exhibited was like compensation for their big body. But as a result of the shift in culture, things are no longer the same. Everything has changed, and they now get involved in ratchet behaviors.

Mammies can be crazy. You dare not fuck with them, and they can go to any length to prove their point. They can employ any means to win a case. If you are in any fight with a mammy, rest assured that she has won the case. They have very strong personality and can withstand anything coming from the other party, it won't take long before mammies retaliate.

They can fight, if fighting is what you bring to the table. If it is exchange of words, they are good at that. They also believe in getting their fair share by fighting for it. If they perceive cheating coming from any angle, they fight and get that which belongs to them. If care is not taken, they take the one that doesn't belong to them as well.

The only reason Mammies behave properly is that their work takes much of their time. If they work for eight hours in the day, they may come back exhausted and maybe don't have enough time to indulge in ratchet behavior. When they do, they check the time because they need to prepare for work the next day. Sometimes they try to show that they are educated by ignoring calls to exchange words. Mammies are certainly interesting characters.

Employment. Mammies, just like thots, are sporadically employed. They are employed both at the low end and the high end of different sectors. Although they are mostly seen at the low level of the field, they are also at a higher level across different fields. Mammies are more educated than thots, so they have more chances of being employed in different organization and at different levels. At the low end mammies are sporadically employed, but at the high end they are definitely employed.

They are open to self-improvement. They can get better and be promoted in their lines of work. Their education opens up more chances for them to get better jobs in different firms.

They have a medium level of entitlement. This means that they also retain some of their traditional habits, such as cooking and cleaning. But their being able and willing to cook and clean for you depends on how much education they have and how high their rank is in their place of work. Just like the thots, they cook and clean and make attempts to raise their kids, if they have them. The only time they fail to carry out these duties is when they

1. have a higher level of education, or
2. have good-paying corporate jobs.

1. When they have a higher level of education: They don't want to do household chores when they have gone to school and attained a certain level in the educational system. They feel big and think that engaging in cooking and cleaning is descending so low. Remember that she already has high self-esteem, so having a certificate further boosts the ego, making it almost impossible for her to bend down and work at home.

It is possible that she may have been doing these chores in the house before she got employment. Once the status changes, her responsibilities in the house change with it.

I know one mammy who used to do all the house chores, and it amazed me. She would wake up early in the morning, do the dishes, wash and iron, keep the house clean, and wake everyone up to eat. This became her daily routine. Then one day I noticed that she had stopped all that. When I asked questions, I found out that she had gotten her degree. She believed that degree owners did not do house chores, and she stopped doing them.

2. When they have good-paying corporate jobs: We have established that mammies see themselves as demigods. You can imagine what would happen in a situation where they do not just have the certificate but have jobs to back them up. It is not just that they have jobs, but the kind of job they have is one that pays well. That is a plus to their egos. When they are at this level, they think that doing house chores is beneath them. They would never think of cooking, let alone cleaning. Mammies who have well-paying jobs find it difficult to maintain those traditional habits passed down to them once they start seeing money.

They can go far as to say that cooking and cleaning are the man's jobs. Usually, they have been in a long term relationship with the men or are married. They may have been doing the chores before, and all of a sudden, they stop doing them and push it to the man, claiming that it is his duty.

Dudes who marry mammies go through hell while on earth. This is because the women they are married to see them as petty. Women can be crazy, and they do not actually believe things like "Take me as I am" and "Love me just the way I am." They lie to themselves, and they know that. When you fall for it, they take you to be gullible. No matter what women say about themselves, they know how they look. They know when they are too ugly, too beautiful, or manageable. Mammies know what they look like, so they see any man who comes for them as being stupid, because mammies know that those dudes must have seen more good-looking women, slender chicks. After seeing them as stupid, mammies treat the dudes that way. They say, "This dude married me? After seeing at all these fine, skinny chicks, this guy picked me?" The mammies think that if those dudes are able to choose them and marry them despite all those beautiful women, then they must be dummies.

Class Level. The class level of mammies is lower than a thot. They do not have good taste and have poor sense of style. They wear funny-looking clothes. including revealing clothes that do not fit into the occasion. They do not have a good dress sense. Their weave, makeup, and accessories do not depict class despite the fact that they have money to get things they need. Most of them do not look attractive. Only few of them look attractive, but that is when they work out a little bit.

Intelligence Level. These women are highly intelligent. They use their smartness to compensate for their body size. It is difficult to see big girls treated as trophy wives. It is true that they get into relationships and marriages, but they are not able to get into those relationships or marriages where the guys take care of them. They usually fend for themselves while they are in relationships. They work to make money and take care of themselves. The funny thing is that they know they have to work. No one tells them to get a job somewhere and make their money from there.

They are smart enough to know that whatever relationship they have with a guy doesn't mean that the guy will provide for all their needs. As a result of this, they engage themselves in one work or the other from the onset. They are also wise to know when they need to change the type of work they do or their workplace. They are not stagnant; they move and grow with the advent of time if there is need for it.

Ambition Level. The mammies are highly ambitious. They wish to go higher than they already are. They try to get higher education, and they pursue good-paying jobs with their qualifications. They do not relax and enjoy the moment; they struggle to get better. They have dreams and goals. The mammies go to school and get higher education. They also try to get good-paying job, which they get on most occasions. They can be in one position in an establishment but aim for a higher and better position.

They work hard to achieve their goals. They are wise enough to spot distraction and weed out deficiencies. They have goals, so they work hard to achieve those goals. They are also aware that no one is ready to give, so they have to work extra hard to give to themselves.

They are willing to learn. They want to become better. They want to earn more. Therefore if learning is what it takes to get more money and upgrade themselves, they do not mind learning.

They are risk takers. These women are ready to take risks, especially when it has to do with making money. They are not afraid of change. As a matter of fact, they are ready to embrace change. They always hope to make the best out of any situation. They are not out to impress people or anyone around them. They simply want to satisfy themselves and be happy they did it.

They want more. The mammies want more than they already have. They believe they can get more because they were able to get to this level. They see themselves with a lens whereby they can get better than they are. They want to be the best and have the most. They set high targets for themselves.

Mammies can be traditional. Just like the thots, mammies are also traditional by nature, but they are less traditional than the thot. This is because once they get their education or jobs, they are likely to leave those things they used to do. Their level of being traditional is dependent on their level of education and the type of jobs they do.

Hustle. The mammies hustle hard for their money. They get different jobs in different sectors to get more money. They go to school to acquire more certificates that they can use in securing jobs with better pay. Although mammies are hustlers, they do not hustle more than the thots because although they can easily get jobs because of their level of education, thots are not educated like they are, so they do dirty jobs to make ends meet. But the fact that mammies get these jobs easily does not mean that they are unserious about it. They carry out their duties efficiently while working on upgrading themselves for promotion.

Traditional Type. If not for cultural or social programming, if things were to go back to the way they were decades ago, the mammy would have been a big mama. She would be a woman who wears dresses that fit a big woman properly, and she'd carry herself in a different way. She would be more decent than she is today. The mammy would have a better attitude and motherly qualities.

IMPLICATIONS OF DEALING WITH A MAMMY

I'm sure you have met that big black woman who carries herself as if she is the only woman who exists. The mammy shares so many similarities with the thot. She has convinced herself beyond a doubt that she is normal while at this size and shape. This conviction has formed how she views herself. She wears clothes that are out of place, and she still takes pride in them because no matter what she looks like, men are bound to flock around her. Even if she wears the most inappropriate dress for an occasion, she will get a good number of stalkers.

These chicks are traditional: they know how to do the house chores, and they do them. But when they get their higher education or secure a good job, that is the end of being traditional. They go to the extent of passing the responsibility to the men with whom they are in a relationship.

She can be employed in a cooperate organization because she is educated. She is the kind of woman where her daily routine is known by everyone. She leaves the house in the morning for work and comes back late in the evening. She can bear children and take care of her children. She does not wait for her man to take care of her—she hustles for her money.

These women find it difficult to give their husbands or boyfriends their place in the home. They do not regard these men well. If you try to get into a relationship with this chick, be rest assured that she will take the head of the family from you. If you are really interested in being the man and the head of your family, then you need to avoid dealing with a mammy.

These women always have men flocking around them because of the following.

1. Their pronounced body assets
2. Black men's willingness to settle
3. The big mama effect

1. Their Pronounced Body Assets

These chicks are not attractive. The fact that they are big highlights the sensitive parts of them, like the breasts and the butt. We know that men are drawn by what they see. When they see these women, they find it difficult to resist initiating a conversation. These chicks know this, and they leverage it to wear any kind of clothes they deem fit, not minding whether it is appropriate. You need to be extra careful about these women because they can attract you with their figure, which is common in the hood.

2. Black Men's Willingness to Settle

Black men are known for their willingness to settle for less when it comes to relationships. They usually think that other people are better than them and should go for the best. They therefore settle for what is left. This is mostly because they have unlimited resources to take care of these women. They go for the ones they can afford, not knowing that they are buying problems for themselves with the little money they have. These big ladies know that the dudes are giving them shit by professing love to them. They know that those men would choose the slim chicks over them, and they try to deal with those men who are caught in their trap accordingly.

3. The Big Mama Effect

The image of the big mama that the dudes are used to can make them feel a strong attachment with this big woman. They hope that after all the comfort they got from their big mama, they are able to get it from this woman because she has a similar look.

WHY SHOULD YOU AVOID THE MAMMY?

Now that we have successfully described the mammy, I assume that you are able to recognize one whenever you see one. I am going to give you the reasons you need to avoid mammies. The black man needs to run from this kind of women because

1. he needs to save his reputation, and
2. he may lose his title as the head of the family.

1. **Save your reputation**. You need to avoid these chicks for principle's sake. Black men have this reputation of being the garbage men of the dating world. In the stratified dating world, the black man is the lowest in the pyramid. They are believed to choose when others have chosen. If there are pretty girls in the vicinity, the black man will only take what remains after others have made their choices. This picture of a black man when it comes to dating is not a good one. Going with the big ladies further consolidates this notion that black men go for the remnants. Of course, whatever that has remained after people have

picked from the most of options is not good. Black men should save their names and their faces by not dating or marrying this kind of woman, because doing so is invariably saying that they went for what was available.

Also, black men are considered to have low self-esteem. They think low of themselves, believing that they cannot do better. They cannot go for the hot and sexy chicks because they may be rejected. They may also believe they do not have the money to maintain the pretty, slender ones. In order to cut their coat according to their cloth, they go for the fat ladies. You can see a man admiring a beautiful chick in the hood, watching her closely without her noticing. Sometimes he knows what her daily routine looks like, but he cannot initiate a conversation with her. He will tell you that those kinds of chicks are for guys with dough. It is funny that after admiring tons of slender chicks, they end up marrying the large ones.

Staying away from this kind of woman is a way of debunking the notion that people have nursed over time. It is a way of telling them that black men cannot tolerate anything or that they make their decisions because of low self-esteem. They rather make their choices about women because that is what their hearts desire.

You need to avoid this woman to save your face and tell the world that you are not going to settle for the less. Go for something better. Do not fall in line with the already known assumption. Prove that a black man can get any woman of his choice.

2. **You are at the risk of losing your crown as the head of the family.** We all know that the man is supposed to be the head of the family. A man who gives orders in the family is the head of the family. The thot allows for this kind of man; she never thinks of dominating the boyfriend or the husband. But with the mammy, it is a whole different story. The mammy may be submissive initially, but once she gets her higher level of education or gets any job that pays her well, she won't

mind taking that crown from you. She makes you her errand boy if she can. She will leave the chores for you and expect you to take care of the babies while she faces her work.

She sees you, who left the pretty ones to marry her, as dumb, and she doesn't hesitate to express it whenever an opportunity calls for it. Remember that the mammy is highly intelligent, so she employs different techniques to get you to serve her. The bad part is that you may be serving her without knowing it, thinking that you are showing that you love her while she is using you. At the end of the day, she is making decisions while you are implementing them.

HOW DO YOU DEAL WITH THE MAMMY?

It may be very difficult to be in a relationship with a mammy or marry her without issues coming up. The best thing to do is to avoid them entirely, but they can be managed. Some men have successfully stayed with this type of women for a very long time, and they have been able to manage the situation.

The following actions can help you stay with the mammy and make the best out of the relationship.

1. Hustle to make money.
2. Remind her constantly that you are the head of the family.
3. Help her do the chores.
4. Encourage her to work out.
5. Provide for her if you have the resources.

1. Hustle and make money. Generally, men go for the big ladies because they cannot afford the slim and pretty ones. But when you make money on your own before venturing into the relationship or marriage, no one thinks that you went for them as a last resort or to save yourself some expenses.

Also, the chick knows that you are not just a random guy without some money. Whether we want to believe it or not, money enforces submissiveness on people. If you have money, more people are ready to do your bidding. You have more friends and more followers. The mammy is no different. You may get the mammy to submit to you by making money.

2. Remind her constantly that you are the head of the family. From time to time, remind her that there are certain things she shouldn't do, and there are some things she should do. Always remind her that you are partners and you are supposed to work together instead of apportioning duties. Do not stomach all the shit coming from her in silence. If you do not react, she will try another one that is worse than before.

From your actions and reactions, let her understand that you are the head of the family and as such deserve some respect from her. You can do this in a mild way or otherwise, depending on the situation. All human beings have a conscience. If you continue like this for a while, she may see to reason with you and put a stop to her attitude. Note that in trying to prove your point as the head of the family, using physical force such as beating and hitting is not a good idea.

3. Help her do the chores. Helping her with the house chores is another method you can use to conquer a mammy, if you utilize it properly. When you start living together as a couple, you may not let it be her sole duty to cook and clean. You can offer to help her. You may not do the difficult part, but be part of the exercise. Let it be something you do together so that at the end of the day, when she gets her job, she won't leave it entirely for you because you also have your job. This means that if you have the same responsibilities, keep your job and take care of the house together so no one feels cheated. Both of you now have the same routine of leaving the house in the morning and coming back later to deal with the chores in the house. If you continue this way, you will see that she will not complain about having so much to do.

4. Encourage her to work out. It may shock you that your large wife or girlfriend has never thought of doing something about her size because you have not mentioned it. You can encourage her to work out or go on a diet. To further ensure the consistency of what she is doing, you may be her coach. Follow her to morning jogging, tell her she is doing something well, and encourage her to do more. If you think she is eating too much, tell her why she needs to reduce the intake and follow up as she makes progress. You will be amazed at the results. Also, put it at the back of your mind that she can resist this. She may say, "I don't have to work out. I am sexy the way I am." Use what she likes to draw her into working out. You can promise her a gift if she meets a target that you set for her.

5. Provide for her if you have the resources. One of the major reasons mammies do shit to their men is because they believe the men don't give them anything. Because he gives her no money, he has no right to tell her what to do, especially when she starts making her own money. You can prevent this feeling from growing inside the mammy by providing for her even when she is working. If she mentions something she needs, get it for her. Buy her gifts and remind her that she is your soul mate. If you are able to provide what she needs, and she sees it herself, it won't be long before that feeling of seeing you as a stupid person for making her your choice dies down. I bet she will never think of dragging you down after that.

If you make all these attempts and she still proves impossible, I think it is time to call it quits because she is delusional and may suck your blood if you do nothing about it.

CHAPTER 3

THE HOOD RAT

By now, I am sure you have started identifying the thots and mammies around you. The thot and the mammy are two sides of the same coin. The only thing is their size difference: if a thot is big, she will behave like a mammy; if a mammy has a small stature, she will behave exactly like a thot. Becoming overweight changes your personality and makes you operate differently.

Many people confuse the hood rat for the thot, but they are two different types of women. Some men have rolled with just the hood rat and have concluded that all black chicks are either hood rats or thots. But they are not the same. This is one of the objectives of this book: to bring to light the different archetypes so that you can identify them and know how best to associate with them.

The hood rat has her own specific characteristics. You can easily spot her upon first meeting. The hood rat is less common than the thot. Unlike the thot and the mammy, the hood rat is not seen in their numbers around the hood. It may sound weird that there are fewer hood rats in the neighborhood. The hood rat is worse than a thot. She can mess up your life at a higher degree. The hood rat will ruin your life beyond repair.

Hood rats are the original ho archetype. We usually attribute thots as hos; even their name implies that. Their promiscuous nature also gave reasons for why they are referred to as hos, but technically they are not really hos because despite their sexual escapades with men, they aren't being paid for sex. Even when they let those men bang them at every corner, they do not get paid.

In past decades, you could find out the woman who was a slut or a tramp, and you could discover that the chick was a hood rat. The only reason we have women today who are displaying ho tendencies is that we have a culture that has made being a ho popular. That is why we have so many women putting up ho characteristics, but they are not actually hoes. The hood rat is the original ho; she is the original source from where others draw their ho nature.

FEATURES OF A HOOD RAT

A hood rat can be identified by the following characteristics.

Appearance. Hood rats usually fit the archetype of being slim or a little bit plump. It is difficult to guess their age by looking at them because they look younger most times. They have a way of making themselves look younger than their age so they can attract men and deceive them as they wish. They always use makeup and weaves to complement their dressing. Their bodies are their workplace, so they take care of it to entice clients.

They are usually tatted. These women use tattoos on different parts of their bodies, especially those parts that can easily be seen, such as their legs, arms, or necks. They usually appear in revealing clothes, not minding whether the outfit fits them. You see them in outfits that look like bikinis so that their tattoos can be seen.

In trying to understand hood rats, it is important that we know the psychology behind tattoos so we can form a better mental picture of this type of woman.

1. **Reconstructing one's image.** People see tattoos as a way of remodeling a human body from a blank canvas and making it look the way the owner wants it. It is similar to getting plastic surgery so that one feels better about oneself. The owner of this tatted body feels better than she did before getting the tattoo. Also, people believe that getting tattoos make them easily noticed, and therefore they look attractive. Instead of noticing someone for her beauty, the tattoo becomes a center of attraction. The tattoo is now the central image of the person's body.

It is possible that they have used their tattoos to redefine themselves, giving themselves the shape they want for themselves. The tattoos help boost their confidence, and they have a better view of themselves.

2. **Sense of belonging.** As long as human beings exist, they belong to a group. Many gangs use a particular tattoo to mark themselves as members of such a group. Not all cliques of people with tattoos are criminals. As a matter of fact, many people who join the army get tattoos in the course of their military service. Sailors are the first recorded people to come back home with tattoos as souvenir after spending time in a foreign land. A post on the army's website shows that an estimate of 90 percent of soldiers have at least one tattoo.

The hood rats feel like they belong due to having these tattoos. They feel comfortable around those bad people with whom they associate.

3. **Less anxiety about death.** People with tattoos are the kind of the people who live in the moment. They do not worry about what happens in the future. I am sure that before they went to get the tattoo, a thought

must have crossed their minds, or a concerned friend asked them what they hoped to do in the near future when they get older and their skin starts to sag. But they do not care. They have gotten what they wanted at this point in time, and the long-term implications are not their concern.

The founder of Project Semicolon, Amy Bleuel, encouraged people suffering from thoughts of taking their lives, anxiety, or depression to draw a semicolon on their hands to remind them that any difficult situations in someone's life has a period. Life continues and will get better by the day. She told them that they were the authors of their lives and therefore should not end it. She encouraged them to live and hope for better, and they will be happy they did it.

In the case of hood rats, they are also known as people who live and enjoy the moment. They do not care what happens tomorrow if their actions boomerangs; it does matter.

4. **They are thrill seekers and risk takers.** Before the present day, in the early 1900s, the major place people went to get tattoos was the circus. People became tatted because they believed it was more fascinating than sideshow attractions and rides. Carnival workers used to have lots of tattoos, and almost every show had an artist who would tattoo members of the public for a fee.

Several studies have shown that people with tattoos are very likely to take risks in their lives. These people are prone to engage in risky behaviors. A tatted person has a higher chance of smoking cigarettes, which of course increases the risk of developing lung cancer. In getting a tattoo, the person knows that there is a moment when the artist is not doing a good job, but going under the needle is a taking a risk, and at the end of the day, the artwork won't come out as imagined. There are so many horrible tattoos out there, and it started with a person who was willing the take the risk.

A hood rat is ready to take risks. All the activities she gets into are risky ventures, but she is thrilled. She enjoys it because that's her nature.

5. **Uniqueness.** Research has shown that people with tattoos show similarities. They generally want to be unique. They want to explore life and experience things outside the norm. They want to be different from people who follow a restricted, rule-following path.

A hood rat, once she opened to someone she trusted, She told him that she got a tattoo on her body because it made her different. It was something that singled her out. She was not like others, and it made her happy. It would be difficult to see someone with the same tattoo in the same position. Even if you see the same artwork, it wouldn't be on the thigh. It may be on the neck or somewhere else, but definitely not on the thigh like hers. That feeling of being unique made her have a better perception of herself.

The irony is that the same people who get tattoos go back to remove them along the line, especially women. Men believe that it continues making them feel better about themselves. In 2006, dermatologist Myrna L. Armstrong polled 196 women who wanted to remove their tattoos. They were asked why they got the tattoos in the first place and why they wanted them removed. The leading answer was that they got the tattoos to feel unique, but by the time they turned thirty, they didn't want them anymore. The leading answer to why they wanted the tattoos gone was they were getting embarrassed as they got older.

Hood rats want to be unique. They want their uniqueness to speak for them. They want to be noticed wherever they go.

6. **Anger.** Professor Viren Swami, from Anglia Ruskin University, conducted a study in 2015. In his study, he found out that the more tattoos people had on their bodies, the angrier they were. He discovered that people with so many tattoos on their skin were known to be violent and verbally aggressive, and they would rebel against authority. Professor

Swami asked them how they would react if someone in a position of authority yelled at them. They were given the options of standing there to accept the scolding, yelling back at the person, or waiting for the person in authority to finish before they responded. Most of the people with tattoos stated that they would not take anything similar to disrespect, and they would react immediately by yelling back.

Dr. Kirby from *Psychology Today* sees some of the violent images people get tattooed as subtle symbols that stem from the inner anger. She considers tattoo a "passive aggression."

It is not proven whether hood rats are quick to anger, but they are usually aggressive. They do not stomach disrespect or anything that looks like it.

7. **Sexually Active.** A study from the Medical University of Silesia proves that people with tattoos (especially women) are more sexually active than people without tattoos. Questionnaires were issued to a large group of people within the age bracket of twenty to thirty-five. The questionnaire was based on their sexual behavior, number of sexual partners, the sexual harassment they have experienced, and how they view themselves as sexually attractive.

The study shows that people with tattoos engaged in sexual behavior earlier in life and at a younger age than those without tattoos. They did not just experience it and stop—they engaged in it more often with their partners. This does not mean that having tattoos makes someone more promiscuous than others; rather, it makes them feel sexy and more confident with their bodies.

Hood rats are no exception. They enjoy sex and use it to make money for themselves.

Attractiveness. These chicks are moderately attractive but dangerously promiscuous. Hood rats are more attractive than thots and mammies.

Their beauty ranges from being very attractive to being very unattractive. They are usually on either side of the spectrum. They do not stay on one end for long. Let us say a particular ho looks very unattractive. It wouldn't take much time before she gets to the other end of the spectrum. This is a sign of hood rats' extreme volatility. They are unpredictable sometimes. Their promiscuous nature is second to none. They bang every dude and do not discriminate regarding the guys they sleep with in the hood. When you hear a chick saying that she has lost count of how many men she sleeps with in a day, that lady is a hood rat.

They are also loud. Being reserved is one attribute a hood rate does not possess. The following characteristics come together to form a loud hood rat.

1. **They are overopinionated.** Everyone knows what they are thinking. They may think they said something about a particular thing to someone, but Their inability to keep their mouths shut and the volume of their voice make it easier for people to know exactly what they're thinking.

2. **They are good at making decisions for people.** Hood rats are not only good at making their own decisions and being snappy about it, but they also find it very easy to make decisions for other people around them. They easily offer to help you decide which action to take. They say, "Are you confused on which color to take? Go ahead with the white one." Not only do they make these decisions easily, but they also are not afraid to voice that decision to everyone, and they are ever ready to fight anyone who disagrees with them.

3. **Their laughter is usually the loudest.** Hood rats do not care about who is there and who is not. They are not interested in whom they are disturbing with their loud voice or laughter. Whenever you see a cluster of people discussing and laughing, listen attentively: one person's laughter is always the loudest, and

that is likely to be a hood rat. People always know when hood rats are around because they know that laughter.

4. **Many people find them intimidating**. Hood rats are known to associate with everyone in the hood, both those ones who are at the top of society and the others who are down. Their ability to mix freely with both levels make some people uncomfortable. The fact that they are also willing to voice their opinions without checking who's around also makes people feel intimidated. Most times when they give their suggestions openly, other people find it hard to refute it for fear of being openly attacked.

5. **Their expressions are loud.** A hood rat's voice is not the only loud thing. Their expressions are loud too. They do not need to talk for people to hear them. Even in their quietness, their expressions speak loudly. People know when they are happy and when they are sad. It is easy to detect when they support something and when they are against it, regardless of whether or not they say it.

Activities. Just as the name implies, hood rats are like the rats in the hood. The hood rat knows herself in and out in the hood. She knows everybody and others' abilities. She knows whom she can meet if she needs help and whom she can step on and go scot-free. She is used to the ghetto life and will not fit into any other lifestyle. It is difficult to get a chick who is a hood rat to change herself into another person. She is comfortable with the kind of life she leads.

Hood rats are familiar with the hood and its environment more than any other type of chick. They therefore take delight in breaking social norms because they know their way out. They are known to be involved in illicit acts, ranging from doing drugs to illicit relationships.

- **Doing drugs.** Drugs are unlawful and not legally permitted, yet a hood rat does not mind and can be involved in trafficking and taking drugs. She knows where to go and what to do when the environment seems unsafe. A hood rat is a side chick to the drug lords.

- **Illicit relationships.** Before marriage, there is no law guiding any romantic relationship, even if it is unethical, such as having a boyfriend and still sleeping with another guy. But once it becomes marriage, having any external affair is unlawful and therefore not permitted by law. Hood rats get themselves involved in illicit relationships, such as sleeping around with married men and lots more. These chicks use sex to their advantage. They can sleep with anyone in power to get to their enemies.

If you ever hear of any illicit activity in the hood, and there are women involved in the shit, those women are likely to be hood rats.

They run the gamut of the hood activity. They are always aware of any information that concerns their hood. They know a new occupant, and they know who just packed out. They are aware of the next social gathering, the venue, and more. If you need information about anything happening in the hood, the hood rat is the best person from whom to get such information.

They are adventurous. They want to explore lives outside their immediate environment. They do not think of how risky it can be for the educated men or the men with class. The normal guys in the hood do not even deal with these chicks because they already know what they are capable of doing. Even the thugs and niggas in the hood do not fuck with the hood rats. It is only those ones who are considered to be dumb.

You will never associate with this kind of chick and go home the same. Once you roll with them, be rest assured that something is going home with you. The tragedy of it is that what is going with you will be something negative. You will go home with whether a basket case or a disease.

1. **You may go home with a basket case.** They can get you involved in deep shit by merely associating with them. If you are lucky, it will be an issue you would survive, but you may not live to tell the story.

I know a dude who tried. He said he was in love with a hood rat and tried showing her that he really was in love. People warned him, but he insisted. That day, the chick opened the door of her apartment for him, and that was unusual. They enjoyed each other's company and had sex. Not long after that, some men burst into the room, took the lady away, and held him down. They gave him the beating of his life, forcing him to say that he would never come across her path again. They told him that she was their property, and no common guy was to have anything to do with her. For committing this offense, they charged him to pay a certain amount. Later that night, they let him go, but not without warning him of the consequences of not paying up. They kept visiting him until he paid off his fine. He didn't have the money at that time, so he had to borrow the money to save his head.

He learned the hard way. Cases like this, and even worse, are what you should expect while dealing with a hood rat. If you are not careful, you may get seriously injured while dealing with this kind of woman.

2. **You may go home with a disease.** As I stated earlier, a hood rat must leave an imprint with you. You may think you have fled from her shackles, but then you may need to go for a medical checkup. If she didn't give you headache in the form of issues, then you may have contacted diseases from her. Some of them have sexually transmitted infections that can cost a fortune to be cured—that is, if they are curable. Hood rats do not mind sharing diseases with anyone they want to punish.

Samson's gonorrhea was not from birth. He got it from a very popular chick in the hood. Even then, I knew she was a hood rat. He had been seen spending quality time with her. Then she parked out of the neighbor, and everything changed. He thought he was going to miss her, and he longed to be with her. Then he went to check himself. He discovered he had gonorrhea. He swore he was going to pay her back, but he couldn't do that anymore.

Hood rats do not give a fuck who you are. They deal with you and get away with it. Initially, you may think that you are using them, but they know what they are doing. Once they get their target, they strike, leaving you with a basket case or taking your time and money.

A hood rat has no shame. A hood rat is a living contradiction. This is because those people normally shy away when some topics are brought up for discussion, especially if it has to do with what they do. For instance, people who do human trafficking may not want to admit it in the presence of a large crowd. A hood rat does not care; she has sold out her shame. She actually takes pride in what she does, even when she knows that it is extremely shameful.

This is that type of chick who is always ready to fight other chicks—and while in the process of fighting them, she reminds them that she is a slut and therefore is more experienced. Hood rats tell you that they sleep with a large number of men in a day, and by the end of the week, they have lost count of how many men with whom they have slept with.

A hood rat admits what she does without shame. She tells you the job description, if you are willing to listen. You hear her say shit like, "Yeah, I am ho. I am a good ho. You fucking do your business, and do it well. I do my own business, and I do it well. I know I am a bitch, but I am a good bitch." She can get into public arguments about sucking dick, and she is not ashamed of it.

A hood rat genuinely has no atom of shame left in her. She is the kind of girl on whom men would run a train on. By this, I mean a group of dudes who are friends can sleep with her, and she will admit it out without shame. She feels proud that she is able to run the crew. In fact, she will praise herself for having the guts and energy to sleep with that circle. If you care to get the details of the story, you can meet her, and she will be ready to give you the information in bits. Some people call her the scum of the universe. The funny part is she always has an audience to herself—people who are willing to listen to her stories.

She wants everyone to be comfortable with what she does, and she can go into a detailed story of her encounter with her clients. She can tell you how she was giving a dude head beside the staircase, or she will give you a detailed story of what happened between her and the dude she met at the club. You go crazy and think, "This is too much information. I do not think I can carry this," but hood rats see it as nothing. This goes to prove that she has no shame. Whether it is doing drugs or selling pussy, a hood rat takes pride in doing it, and she readily reminds you of the shit she does if you look like you have forgotten it.

I cannot remember how I got into a conversation with one of them. I was enjoying fresh air outside with a cup of coffee, and she came over. We got to talking, and I asked her what does she do for a living. She outright told me that she sells pussy. I was shocked. What would give a woman such confidence to tell a stranger that she was a slut? That was an anomaly, but not for a hood rat. She didn't waste time to venture into stories regarding her escapades with men. She told me how she made her first hundred dollars, and she continued until I interrupted her stories.

Self-Esteem. A hood rat has high self-esteem and low self-esteem at the same time. This may sound weird, but some people possess different self-esteem in different situations. A child may be good academically, meaning that the child enjoys doing anything related to school work; whenever it comes to class work, you will see that the child will have a lot of confidence. On the other hand, this same child may not be good at engaging in social behavior. This means that the child doesn't easily make friends or go out to meet people; The child would therefore have low self-esteem in that regard.

A hood rat has a combination of high self-esteem and low self-esteem. This is a result of cultural programming versus traditional morality. I have observed that they have this dual self-esteem at the same time.

> **High self-esteem.** When it comes to what they do and how they manage themselves out of situations, hood rats hold themselves to very high esteem. They do not mind who is listening or looking at them. They announce that they have a dick they need to attend to, not minding how you take it. They also believe they can deal with anyone who steps on their toes, and this notion boost their confidence. They are proud that they are messing with men they are not supposed to get close to.

> **Low self-esteem.** Hood rats are considered to have low self-esteem because if they had more confidence in themselves, they would think better of themselves and wouldn't sink so low as to sell their pussies. The shit they are involved in is real shit, and someone with high self-esteem would not dare to do it. Only a woman with low self-esteem would lower herself to do such shit. This contradicting personality is why I call the hood rat a living contradiction.

Children. Hood rats try as hard as possible to avoid having children. They are aware of the various ways they can have sex yet won't get pregnant: they use of contraceptives, the safe and unsafe periods, and more. They practice these methods so as to not conceive. They do not want children because having children around can disturb the kind of work they do. Unlike the thot and mammy, who makes attempts to raise their children, the hood rat does not put raising children in her schedule.

Hood rats do not consider raising children because of the following reasons.

1. It eats into their time.

Whether full time or part time, being a mother would steal the time they were supposed to use for business. From the time the pregnancy starts showing, they won't be getting clients as usual. Even if they do, the clients are likely to leave them once they discover that they are pregnant. Also, they won't be as strong as they used to be to attend to those social misconducts. The money and adventure they miss during this period is something they do not want to experience. In order to not see themselves in this kind of situation, they make every attempt to not have kids.

2. They would have to get a place to stay.

Typical hood rats do not have apartments to themselves. If they had kids, they would have to stay with somebody—a friend or a relative. Having kids would therefore, mean that they have to get a decent apartment to comfortably accommodate the newborn, which they are not willing to do. They prefer not having a child than being in this kind of situation.

3. They would have to provide for children.

A hood rat is aware that having children comes with some many responsibilities, and that is exactly what she is running away from. She does not want to think for herself, let alone think for another person as well. She is not cut out for performing motherly roles. She knows that if she has children, it means she has to take care of them, see to their welfare, and provide food and other necessary things for the child. Hell, no! The hood rat would never do these things. She prefers her freedom so that she can go anywhere and at any time without having to think about anybody.

Tanisha is a hood rat who is well-known in the hood for her sexual involvement with men. She fits all the descriptions of a hood rat. She has no house and stays with her friend. I am not sure of how many years her friend has housed her, but I do know that she stays out of the house more than she's there. On most occasions, she goes to a hotel with her new customers, or she goes to their houses. She usually comes back with stories of her adventures. Her friend has tried talking to her about her lifestyle and the possibility of her getting pregnant, but she bragged that she can never get pregnant. Her friend reminded her that she lacked the means to take proper care of the child if she eventually gave birth, but the hood rat wouldn't listen.

It didn't take much time for her to miss her period. They conducted a test, and it came out positive. She tried to abort the baby, but it proved more stubborn than the mother. She had to carry the pregnancy. Throughout that period, she kept ranting about how she had lost her customers and couldn't wait to go back to business. She was always on the phone, taking calls and replying to messages. True to her word, immediately after she gave birth, she called the child bad news and left the house. She hadn't been seen since she gave birth to that child.

In general, having children limits hood rats' activities. It is difficult to be a hood rat and stand for what it represents when you have kids to take care of. On few occasions, these methods they use to avoid pregnancy may fail. In such cases, they birth these children but never take care of them. They drop their babies with anyone who cares to take them. They may try to scare the children away by depriving them of their rights or opening up by telling them to go anywhere they wish. They feel they are being punished for having children around, and they would not try to raise the kid the right way. They do not care whether the children eat or change clothes. They simply abandon their children. They can also pass children to relatives, such as their cousins, mothers, aunts, or grandmothers, depending on who is willing to take the child. If everything else fails, the hood rat does not mind taking her children to the orphanage.

At the end of the day, their offspring turn out to be a nuisance because of the kind of upbringing they had. You can identify these children because they behave like animals that are unleashed, and they don't care about anything in the world. They can be spontaneous and do things that come to mind without giving a second thought. They behave as if they don't think and don't care about the people around him. They are as crazy as anyone. A hood rat is the mother of such creatures. Children raised by women like this turn out to be headaches in society.

THE IMPLICATIONS OF NEGLECTING THEIR CHILDREN

The implications of neglecting a child's need cannot be overlooked. The hood rat plays a role in forming a child that is not whole, lacking in so many angles. When the children finally become adults, the results start showing. It is later in life that the harm done to the children becomes significant due to the cumulative nature of neglect and unhealthy exposure. Children raised by a hood rat are likely to suffer from some or all of the following.

1. **Behavioral problems.** A hood rat does not have the best of character. She cannot raise a child the proper way, even if she tries not to think of a situation where she outright rejects the child. The child is likely to grow up not knowing his left nor his right. He may not know what is morally wrong or what is traditionally wrong. He does not have a strong personality makeup because he has no principles. He only does want he feels like anytime he wants. This is because the mother did not teach him the right things to do and at what time.

2. **Depression.** Hood rats makes childhood unbearable for their children. Children grow up thinking that life is that way. They fail to visualize bright futures. They are not happy with the kind of lives they lead, and they have no enthusiasm in life.

3. **Low self-esteem.** These children usually have low self-esteem because they do not have what other children of their age do. Their mothers did not give them the opportunity to enjoy life with a mother, and it is telling in their self-esteem. They cannot do what others are doing because they feel they do not belong to their class.

While the children are going through this psychological state, the hood rat is somewhere riding a dick, emptying some bottles, or partying hard. This is why I say that she is worse than a thot. You have seen that thots do not operate this way—they would ensure that there children has a place to call their own. Maybe thots would be in a long-term relationship and take care of their own children. Although she may mess around with dudes, a thot would never abandon her kids.

Marriage. Hood rats do not stay in long-term relationship, let alone marriage. They see long-term relationships as a waste of time. If they are loyal to one man, they cannot get the same amount of money or attention they get from sleeping around with many men. A hood rat views being in this relationship as something that is stealing the little time she has for her business. The time she spends caring for one boyfriend or husband would be time lost making cash from different men.

Being in a long-term relationship means that she would be committed to a particular man, and she is not ready to give in to that kind of shit. To her, a long-term relationship or marriage is a prison where you do not get to do whatever you please because you do not want to hurt the guy involved. She would rather enjoy her freedom and make money while she's at it.

The longest relationship a hood rat has is with a pimp. This is possible because the pimp understands her line of business and can send her to his clients if the need arises. But then, this relationship is only possible if she has a pimp.

While in this situation, marriage is not for hood rats. They do not consider marriage for any reason. Marriage is like closing their business, which they are not ready to do. As a married women, they cannot meet their clients anymore, and they wouldn't even have time to make trouble with people.

Attitude. Hood rats have more attitude than thots and mammies combined. They suffer from extreme manic behavior. They have a tendency to flare up at the slightest provocation, and they can be physically violent. Everything to them can be resolved with fighting. If you challenge them publicly, they will fight you. If they smell disrespect, they will fight. Anyone who is dealing with them needs to be ready to fight at all times.

Hood rats make a suggestion in a meeting and expect everyone to buy their ideas. Once they perceive that anyone is countering their suggestion, that person should be ready for what comes afterward, which of course is fighting.

Employment. You can hardly hear of this type of chick being employed in a corporate organization. They cannot work in such establishments because they do not have the educational qualifications. Not only that, but they cannot fit in. They have a crazy lifestyle, and giving them work is like punishing them. If you ever hear that they are employed, it is usually as strippers or prostitutes, and that is at the low level.

This is the type of chick that you see in a low-class strippers' club—the type that only a few classless people patronize. It is true that they make money from their stripper business, but it is not the kind of money that other strippers make. They make this little sum because of the kind of people who come to where they work. The bigger circles with class go for a higher end, whereas the people at the bottom of the category go to a place they can afford. It is this set of people that hood rats meet in their "places of work." Hood rats can be in a hotel and be doing all sorts of shit for forty bucks. That's how low they operate.

A hood rat can be very mean when it comes to business. Remember that she is very violent. She can stab your ass if you fail to pay her as agreed, after she has finished rendering her service. She expects that after you have agreed with her on a certain amount, you are to stand by your words and pay once she has completed the task. If you fail to do the needful, then you have something else coming.

She can set you up to achieve her aim of punishing you. This is the type of chick who can set you up to be robbed or beaten. She can plant bait for you, and when it catches you, she eats you raw. If you are an educated man or a man with class, the hood rat looks at you like something to eat. She can plot ways to milk you of your resources. She may set you up, hold your loved ones ransom, get you locked up, get you killed, or threaten you. She will ruin your life—all in a bid to get money from you.

Level of entitlement. Hood rats possess no concept of entitlement. They have nothing to do with house chores such as cleaning and cooking. They would not notice that their children are starving. They do not even have static homes.

Simply put, a hood rat is the lady who wakes up in the morning and leaves the house. She doesn't care whom she is leaving behind in the house; whether it is her child or a friend, it is not her problem. Whether she finds something to eat for the day, that is not what she thinks about. As long as she has dressed up, checked herself in the mirror, and seen that she is looking good, she is out. She goes to hustle for money, jumping from one man to the other and from one end of the hood to the other. Whenever she feels like she needs a break, she goes to a particular joint where she can meet people and have good conversations. When she is done, she goes back to work. She will probably not sleep at home that night. Anytime that business is dull, she may switch to doing drugs. The routine continues every day.

You will see that in this routine, going home to check on her people is not in her agenda. She never considers that. Cooking and cleaning is not the last thing on the list—it is not on the list at all.

Class level. A hood rat has no class. Her class level is very low. The low class is seen all around her, starting with the cheap hair she makes and her cheap tattoos. Inasmuch as they have tattoos all over them, those tattoos are cheap ones. She does not even have a place of her own to boast with, so you cannot access her furniture. They meet cheap men and get paid in low amounts. Whenever she sees a man who looks as if he has money, she wants to strip him of everything he has. She sells her body for a penny or for drugs. She usually follows her client to his house (which normally speaks of anything but class) or to a sketchy, cheap motel.

She is violent. She fights in the hood with anyone who steps on her toes. Once she feels there is a need to fight, she fights. A woman with class would never fight in public, but that is not true for a hood rat. This chick has no remorse for any of this shit she does. She thinks highly of herself despite all these shameful things she does.

Intelligence. A hood rat is not intelligent at all. Her intelligence level is very low. If she were intelligent, she would think of something better than what she is into. She wouldn't brag about her "job."

Ambition level. A hood rat is very comfortable with her clients and what she gets from them. She does not think of trying out any other business or getting a job somewhere. If there is something she thinks about, it is how to strip the new guy who looks rich and how to get more out of those clients she is used to getting.

Hustle. She is a hustler. A hood rat does not have the educational qualifications to apply for cooperate work. It is not like she wants to work there anyway, but she will do anything to make some cash. She can do all sorts of dirty things to make money: she sells her body, sells drugs, steals from people, and conspires with people to set you up and get cash from you.

She can leave the house in the morning to start the day's business and come back anytime in a bid to make money. Money is the first thing on her mind. If she gets a client, she makes sure that they agree on a particular amount before she gives her services. She also ensures that she gets that agreed amount from the client, and if possible, she makes the client give her a tip.

A hood rat knows the hidden corners in the hood that you have never noticed even though you have stayed there for years. She knows who takes hard drugs and who needs them. She can therefore make these drugs available and get her money. Not minding that this venture is risky, this chick ventures into it because she knows that she is going to make some money at the end of the day.

This chick wants money, and she is on the lookout for it. She can steal from her client or any other person. She will spend the night with you, and you will wake up to see that she has gone with your money and your expensive jewelry. She will sell those stolen items in the hood and have some money for herself. She can also be a pickpocket.

A hood rat can conspire with some people to set you up for robbery. She can pay some guys to rob you on your way to work or in your house, and she will be among the pity party. She can do it in such a way that the hoodlums will come in when she is with you and take your money and items. She will share the proceeds with those thieves later, or take the items and pay them off. Yes, a hood rat is this deadly.

You may be thinking that someone who can come up with these tricks is intelligent, but there is a difference between hustle and intelligence. Intelligence depicts the "capacity of mind, especially to understand principles, truths, facts or meanings, acquire knowledge, and apply it to practice; the ability to comprehend and learn." A hood rat lacks in this regard. But by hustle, I mean street intelligence. She has a lot of street intelligence. She knows the best way to survive on the street. She can run games and get away with them.

Lily, one of the few hood rats I know, gets into a lot of shit. You'd think she is going behind bars soon, but she stays around. She smokes and sells hard drugs, but she seems invisible whenever the police come around. Twice they have searched the place she stays, but she has never been found wanting in any way. No exhibit has ever been found in her possession. It was already looking as if she was diabolic until I found out that she always clears the road before the cops come.

She knows her game very well. When it comes to the street, she knows the buttons to press. She can analyze a situation and know the next thing that may happen. She knows when the police are likely to invade the hood, and she clears any materials in her possession that can give her away.

Ratchet level. A hood rat's ratchet level is very high. You do not fuck with this chick because she is going to mess up your life. She won't notice any good things about you. She can pour water on you when you are set to leave the house for your workplace. She can be very nasty, more so than the thot and the mammy put together. She does not care whether it means getting you injured. She is only interested in passing her message to you, and she feels satisfied doing that.

Traditions type. If you take away all the social programming or cultural programming, then back in the days, when these programmings were not around, the hood rat would be a town slut. A town slut is a person who takes delight in attending parties, getting wasted on alcohol or any other related substance, flirting to get drinks and money, and fucking anyone who provides any of those items. She is that chick that parents would use as an example when advising their kids, "You need to take your life seriously. If not, you will end up like …" She is the chick whom everybody looks at in a shameful manner.

WHY SHOULD YOU AVOID THE HOOD RAT

You need to avoid these chicks for obvious reasons. This is for the benefit of the people who come to the hood to talk to chicks. If you are able to identify these traits in anyone, I advise you run for your life because if you mess around with hood rats, they will ruin your life in such a way that you may not be able to pick up the pieces.

1. A hood rat can mess up your life. She will employ every means within her reach to deal with you. She can give you a disease that will last your whole life. She can blackmail you or hold hostage anyone dear to your heart while she extorts money from you. She can set you up, and you can be arrested and thrown behind bars. A hood rat is so mean. At the extreme end, she can kill you if your offense is a huge one.

2. She doesn't mind sleeping with your friends. To this chick, whoring is a habit. She doesn't mind that she has something going on between both of you. She will sleep with your friends without an apology, especially if your friends have some bucks to offer her. You may even think you are dating her, but she sees you as one of her clients. The annoying part of it is that she may be the one to tell you about sleeping with your friends, and she may include the details. She will not regard you as anything important to her.

3. She cannot take care of the home. A hood rat cannot look after human beings and the items in your home. If she eventually gives birth, she ends up scaring away the child or neglecting the child and it's needs. She won't notice your existence. Cooking and cleaning are not her things; she avoids doing such chores. You do not want to roll with a woman who will not take her place as a woman.

4. She has no shame. A hood rat is so proud of what she does. She tells people who care to know about her adventures. She may even tell people how good or bad you are in bed. She can go as far as comparing you with your friends with whom she's slept with. She may tell you that

your friends pay better than you and threaten to follow them. She takes delight in sleeping around and shows no remorse for abandoning her child. She brags with the number of people she has fought with, and she will readily deal with you if you fuck with her.

5. She cannot hold down a decent job. She has acclimatized with her slut business such that doing any other business would be impossible. She enjoys her type of work and wouldn't think of giving herself a break. Little wonder that she wouldn't become a submissive wife and give birth. She cannot bring herself to do decent work. She wants to sell herself. If you roll with this chick, know that you are dealing with a public property, and the ownership can change at any time.

Also, this chick may be talking to a dude you do not know about. If you mess with her, she can ask for help, and her other men may shoot your fucking ass.

A hood rat values no man. She sees men as instruments to achieve her goals. Either she gets money from them, or she relies on the power they wield to manipulate the situation to her advantage.

CHAPTER 4

THE BAD BITCH

The bad bitch is similar to the hood rat. I would say that she is the opposite of the hood rat. The bad bitch and the hood rat are like different sides of the same coin. They are similar in most aspects. The hood rat and the bad bitch share the same relationship that the thot and the mammy share. The bad bitch will ruin your life in the same way the hood rat will ruin your life. So many guys do not see it until it is too late.

Some guys may see a hood rat and may not want to fuck her, but the same guys see a bad bitch and get very interested in her. When a study was conducted on how many people would want to sleep with a hood rat, 75 percent of the people chose no. But then the same question was given for a bad bitch to the same people, and 95 percent said yes.

For these guys who polled that they would sleep with bad bitches, I advise you to stay away from them because they will ruin your life in the same way a hood rat does. The bad bitch has set her own targets and does not care how the target is attained. The only thing she cares about is getting her results.

Bad bitches appear like window dressing:
they have a deceptive outward

appearance. They look so perfect and nice from the outside, but if you come close to them, they will deal with you. Note that there are other chicks in the hood who look good and are not classified as bad bitches. Just because the chick is beautiful does not mean that she is a bad bitch.

There are reasons this one is called a bad bitch. She is not very different from a hood rat except for a few differences. The bad bitch does what she wants, whereas the hood rat does what she can.

Bad bitches represent a very small percentage of women in the hood. The hood rats are few, but the bad bitches are even fewer. This is mainly because they do not remain in the hood for long. They have the potential to leave the hood at any time because they can attract men with more resources who can give them a meal ticket out of the hood.

Regina, one of the bad bitches who used to stay in the hood, didn't stay for long. She is a very beautiful lady—exactly the description of a bad bitch. When she was still in the hood, the kinds of guys who flocked around her were those types that you wouldn't want to compete with because they have both good looks and resources. She stayed in the hood for less than a year before she left. I hear she now stays somewhere in town.

Regina was able to relocate not because she had the money, but because of the kinds of guys she was able to attract with her good looks. She played her cards well because she was so good at it, and she got what she wanted. This does not necessarily mean that bad bitches must get an apartment for themselves outside the hood; they may go out of the hood to stay with any of the guys they are able to attract.

A bad bitch is a dope boy's special. This implies that you must have money to fuck them. They have nothing to do with anyone who does not smell of affluence. This bitch will ruin a dope boy's life the same way the hood rat would ruin an average dude's life. A bad bitch is like a time bomb served in a beautiful vessel. You will be tempted to carry it home, but when it explodes, it consumes everyone involved.

Appearance. The mere sight of a bad bitch tells you that she is bad. You do not need any confirmation to consolidate it. A bad bitch appears in all her glory and charm. She has the right hips and the right breasts, molded and fixed as if they was done by a potter who knows his onions. The bad bitch has this archetype, and you will hear a man say that she is a dime. She has a pretty face, attractive eyes, well-formed lips, and the right curves in the right places. She has an expensive weave, a Coke bottle shape, and flawless skin. She is that type of chick whom those men with class and education are dying to get. They say, "Look at her! She is the one I want. This chick is bad. How do I talk to her? I hope no one is eyeing this chick with me because she is mine. She is a pretty young thing and has no kids. I want her."

She has that type of physique that women admire, not to mention the opposite sex. If you are in the hood with your fellow guys, and suddenly a chick's presence distracts everyone as you all look in that direction, that's the bad bitch. She looks so appealing to the eyes that you do not mind going home with her after the mere sight of her. This chick is hot, and what I call a forbidden fruit.

This is why I had to put up this text. You may see this kind of chick, and you follow her immediately because you have seen someone who appeals to your eyes, unaware that this is not a regular chick. You do not know how they operate and therefore do not know how best to arrest the situation. This is because most guys, on seeing this kind of hot chick, immediately stop using their brains and start thinking with their dicks. It is forgivable, but when you are aware of the kind of chick you have seen, if your dick starts thinking for you, you will regret it sooner or later.

PHYSICAL FEATURES OF THE BAD BITCH THAT DRAWS MEN TO HER

We know that a bad bitch is a beauty to behold, but we do not know to what extent. I will analyze the physical features that make men want to go home with them.

- Their waist-to-hip ratio. The ratio of waist to hip of a bad bitch is very pleasing to the eyes and comes in the right proportions. The big one is not too big, and the small one is not too small.

- A high, melodious voice. A study conducted shows that a high-pitched voice evokes youthfulness, and having a melodious voice portrays a feminine structure. These things attract men. For example, if a call wrongly comes to a phone belonging to a female, the guy is likely to call again if the lady has a good voice. He would never try calling again if her voice was not nice.

- A neat hairdo. This may sound strange, but it is true. Men get attracted to women who have neat hairdos. The way the women keep their hair shows how good they are at taking care of themselves. Full and long hair is usually very attractive and shows a healthy hair. The bad bitch always visits the salon to do her hair and weaves. She appears stunning whenever she makes a visit to the salon, thereby drawing more male attention to herself.

- Charming smiles. I made it known earlier that the bad chick has well-curved lips. You can imagine what would happen when these lips form a smile. Even the strong heart of the wicked king would melt. Their white teeth add to the charm. The smile in itself shows happiness, and happiness is contagious. People who always smile are believed to be happy people. Men therefore get charmed by this smile.

- Good makeup. Men fall for good makeup that blends with the skin and facial structure. I do not mean those funny makeup attempts we see on the faces of a thot and the mammy. The bad bitch, as a classy chick, knows the right tone of makeup that is perfect for her face and complexion, and she applies it evenly. This also attracts men to her.

- Choice of clothes. The fact that a man does not wear all those designers clothes does not mean that he won't admire anyone in that outfit. Most times, men would want their girlfriends or their wives to appear in such clothes. The bad bitch knows the right clothes to wear and when. She knows how to dress to the clubhouse and what to look like if she needs to visit a friend. They have good dress sense, and this adds more men to the number of their admirers. Though most of her clothes are revealing, men like it that way because it accentuates the woman's features.

- Height. It has been proved that taller women are more attractive, and the bad bitch is blessed with this feature. They are usually tall or of average height. It is rare to see a bad bitch who is short.

- Arm length. It has been observed that men prefer tall women with longer arms. They seek out for long legs, but they prefer long and slender arms. Check out these bad bitches, and they all fit this description. I do not know whether they work out to gain these features, but they do have them, and this obviously attracts men to them.

- Well-shaped breast. Their breast are well molded and attractive, not too big and not too small. A narrow waist compliments the moderately sized breasts, and men would kill to have grasp them. Researchers have tracked the eye movement of men when looking at images of women, and men's eyes first go to the breasts and waists. It was noticed that they also look longer on breasts. When they have seen the overall picture, their eyes rest back on the breasts for general assessment. This is also what happens when they see a woman, but the eye movement happens in a flash so that you can't notice it.

- Overall grooming. Men can notice a woman who engages in unhygienic activities from miles away, and it is a turnoff for them. Personal grooming is a hobby for these bad bitches. They dedicate their time to taking good care of themselves and looking good. They do their manicures and pedicures and visit the spa if the need arises. This draws more men, especially from the upper class.

These bitches enjoy this attention given to them by men because that is how they get their clients.

Children. The bad bitch typically does not have any children out of wedlock. She does everything within her power to ensure that she does not have children. This is part of her that attracts men to her. Most men do not want to mingle with a woman who has a child from another man. The fact that this beautiful chick has no children is a credit to her.

Some men tell you that they can only be in a relationship with a beautiful chick, and if she doesn't have a child, that is a plus. A bad bitch fits all these criteria, but what these men do not know is that these chicks are not what they seem to be.

They do not want to conceive because of obvious reasons.

1. It would disrupt her business.
2. It would disfigure her shape.
3. It may scare her clients.
4. It is a distraction to her.

1. **It would disrupt their business**. Having a child means that she would devote her time to taking care of the child. A bad bitch does not need any of these commitments. She cannot be out on her business and be thinking of a child she's left at home. Also, the period of carrying and giving birth to the child spells a long absence from work, and she

does not even want to try. She wants to be available for business at all times and to make more money.

2. **It would disfigure her shape.** Childbearing is a piece of bad news to the bad bitch. It is a known fact that once you give birth, your body does not remain the same. You are bound to have scars on your stomach, an enlarged stomach, and other signs of motherhood. This bitch does not want to get to the point where her body is not sexy anymore because she then can no longer attract clients. Her body is her office, so she needs to keep it in shape, and giving birth to a child would not help in this venture.

3. **It may scare her clients.** Inasmuch as some men do not mind whether a woman has kids, most of them do not really want to associate with a woman who has a child out of wedlock. This bitch makes her money from the attention she is able to drive from males, and having a child can reduce the number of men she gets for herself. A man can feel reluctant about allowing a woman and her child to come and stay in his place, but he wouldn't give it a second thought if it is just the chick.

4. **It is a distraction to her.** Giving birth would make this chick have divided attention. A bad bitch is aware that if she gave birth, she would have to think about her work and another individual, which would be a setback in her business. Whether she would have the child stay with her or pass the child on to another relative does not make the child any less her child. She has to think about the child at one point or the other. She needs to focus on her work and avoid any distractions, and giving birth is a very big distraction to her.

Activities. It is true that the bad bitch is a ho just like the hood rat, but the bad bitch can place a premium on her stripping and prostitution. She can charge any amount she feels like to her clients, and they pay up. A bad bitch can charge between five hundred to a thousand dollars, and those drug dealers will let the money flow. If she discovers that it was very easy for the guy to afford the amount she charged, she will increase it the next time, and desperate guys will pay up to smash this chick because if they don't, other guys are in the queue.

If a bad chick charges about seven hundred bucks and discovers that you didn't find it difficult giving her that amount, then if you come again another time, she will charge you one thousand dollars. This time around, you may not want to discontinue with her. If you try to withdraw, another guy will take over. You may not have the chance to get to her again if you change your mind. She knows that she has a queue of orders, and she leverages this.

She is a premium stripper. If you have ever been to the strip' club, people are dancing and rocking bodies. Then all of a sudden, the disk jockey stops the music to announce a particular stripper, and everyone shifts aside to welcome the stripper. Every other bitch leaves to go to the back room, and every other person in the club is watching that one stripper. That is the bad bitch. She is the premier stripper, the one whom guys come to the club for, make a ring around, and throw money to.

Sometime last week, I was bored and decided to look around. I went to the strip club. The atmosphere was getting livelier by the moment, and I enjoyed the loud music and the dancing. After a time, I joined in the exercise. Not long after I started dancing, the DJ stopped the music and made an announcement. "Ladies and gentlemen, I want you to come to the stage and welcome Sapphire." A bitch appeared looking like a goddess, in all shades of beauty. It didn't take seconds before all the other bitches disappeared. Everybody's attention was focused on this one bitch. I knew immediately that was the bad bitch in her wholeness. Not long after that, the guys circled her and started throwing some money for her.

A bad bitch is not seen in cheap hotels or low-class areas. She makes sure that the client she is following will be able to afford high-class hotels and relaxation centers.

SIGNS THAT THE BAD BITCH COMES WITH AN ULTERIOR MOTIVE

These are signs to show that the bad bitch has come to tear down the resources you have built up over the years. These signs may be subtle to notice, but if you are observant, you will notice these behaviors in her because she cannot hide them for long. She is obsessed with money, not minding whose money it is.

- **The bad bitch pays a lot of attention to her appearance.**

This is the first thing you notice about her. She cares so much about what she looks like at every point in time. You wouldn't be surprised to notice that she carries a mirror around in her bag. She never dares to look ugly or old-fashioned. She never wants people to look at her and think she is poor. Even if she doesn't have money to get food, she must ensure that she follows the fashion trend, wear the latest clothes or handbags, and buy other things that people are currently using.

She makes sure she appears perfect at all times, and she is interested in people's opinions about her, especially people of high class. She will asks you what your friends think about her so she knows how to adjust.

- **The bad bitch loves to shop.**

This chick's hobby is shopping. Once she gets money, the next thing she thinks about is shopping. Now that she has a money bank in the form of a human being, she doesn't need to get the money to shop anymore. She needs your money or your credit card. She spends most of her time shopping, and she forgets that it is someone else funding the shopping. This bitch does not mind shopping every day. It does not really matter whether the things she buys are things she needs. What is important is that she is shopping and spending your money.

- **A bad bitch can never pay her own bills.**

It is almost impossible for this chick to pay her bills. She must ensure that you pay all her bills. She makes it your responsibility to take care of everything that concerns her. She will probably make excuses or persuade you to pay her bills. If you are going out for a cup of coffee, know that the bill is on you.

- **She likes showing off.**

This is a chick who delights in showing off those things she has. She doesn't see anything wrong with this because she needs to let people know that she owns these brand items. She talks about them with her friends and anyone who cares to listen. She announces how much she bought them for and posts numerous pictures of them on social media. The whole world has to know about these assets. Her ego increases as her social media likes increase. It encourages her to show off even more. Guess who is funding these items? Your pocket.

- **She likes the luxurious lifestyle.**

The bad bitch wants to live a luxurious life similar to what celebrities have. She wants to be associated with wealth and status, and somehow she has a way of achieving it by taking from the pockets of whomever she is in a relationship with. She expects the guy to provide her with a lot of money so she can maintain this kind of lifestyle. Once you prove that you are below her expectations, she will leave you for another person who can provide her with what she wants.

- **She loves wealthy men.**

The quality she checks out in men is how rich they are. She is not interested in your personality. As long as your pocket is large enough to accommodate her demands, you are the real man. The quantity of love she has for you is directly proportional to the amount of money you have. If you inform her that you have gone bankrupt today, she will disappear from your life today. She believes that with a rich man by her side, she can live the kind of life she desires. Her days must be filled with exotic vacations and expensive gifts.

- **She only thinks of how to spend money.**

A bad bitch will only give you ideas on how to spend money. You will wonder why she doesn't give ideas for how you should make money. She only brings those suggestions to the table to ensure that she spends your money to the last penny. She doesn't want any money to remain when she is done with you. To her, it doesn't really matter if you are keeping anything for tomorrow or saving for rainy days.

- **She has pride.**

She does not hang out with every Tom, Dick, and Harry. She picks the people she rolls with. She finds her way to get into the rich inner circles, and it is easy for her because of her good looks and the kind of strip clubs she visits. If she must be a part of this world, then she must pay so much attention to her physical outlook by adorning herself with everything possible.

This kind of person will not want any of her friends to look classless and poor. She therefore limits the kinds of people she is seen with so that is doesn't dent her image. Not everyone can ask to meet her. It must be someone from that circle, or someone who is willing to provide any amount of money she needs. If she hangs out with everybody, her premium can be affected. For example, if you know that you have seen a chick with a particular celebrity, you will be willing to pay any amount she charges because you think she is worth it. This is a tactic that the bad bitch employs for one reason: to spend your money to the last dime.

- **She loves accepting gifts.**

A bad bitch's best moment is the moment you shower her with gifts— not just any gifts, but expensive gifts. The more expensive the gifts are, the more love she shows you because she expects another gift to come soon. She doesn't care how you get the money, or whether there is still money after she's gone. You can sell your father's house to buy her a car, and she does not mind. As long as the gifts you buy suit her taste, you are on the same page with her. Do not be deceived that she loves you. She loves the gifts you get for her, not you.

THE RELATIONSHIP BETWEEN A BAD BITCH AND A HOOD RAT

The bad chicks make their pick first because they have good looks. When they are done picking, they pass the crumbs down to the hood rats. The hood rat therefore meet the low-end clients.

Jack, a new guy to the hood, came to check out the chicks. He came with some other guys, but it was as if those guys were sharpshooters. They saw the bad bitches around; there were two at that moment. The chicks had already made their choices at that moment. They chose the first guys who came to talk to them. Jack had to find the next available chick in the hood. The chick was a hood rat.

A bad bitch can make a lot of money stripping. Men usually come to the club to drop money for them, asking them to do one thing for them or another. For example, a dude can pay three hundred dollars to this chick for a lap dance, and another dude will come and pay higher—say, four hundred. It will continue that way till it gets to the peak, and the bitch will go with the highest bidder.

Another difference between the hood rat and the bad bitch is that with the hood rats, you already know that she is out for your money, so you are extra conscious of how you relate with her. The bad bitch does not show any trait of being interested in your money. She looks like someone who is already made and does not care about your own money, but that's not true. She will milk you dry.

A guy I know shared his own experience with this kind of bitch. He said that he was a kind of person who was always meticulous whenever he dealt with women. He had been picking these ladies from the hood for a while, and he was being too conscious of their presence because he knew what they could do. This measure had always worked for him until the day he picked a very beautiful one. He thought she would not be interested in his money because of how she looked, but she kept demanding things. She would make this demand in a way that would be difficult for him to say no. She eventually got everything she wanted.

This guy met two different kinds of chicks, but he didn't know it. The ideas that I am sharing in this book make it easy for you to identify any chick in the hood whom you need to avoid.

With a bad bitch, you are likely to catch a basket case or a disease.

Catching a basket case. A bad bitch can mess you up, but she will do it in such a way that you won't see it coming until she has drawn the last line. She is fighting you and blowing the injured part. You will even enjoy the "biting." A bad bitch can tear down the empire you have built. She will spend all your resources until she is sure there is none left, and then you will no longer see her.

A man picked up one of these bitches from the club. She charged him for the night, and the man agreed to pay. The man told her to request anything she wanted because she was a goddess, and he was ready to serve her. He didn't know that he was only digging his grave. This chick saw that her trap had a lump of big meat, and she was relaxed to enjoy it. This guy took the lady to a very expensive hotel where they knew him very well. The aim was to get this lady enticed to love him more, and he would offset the bill whenever he could.

He didn't know that he had something else coming. He left for work the next day hoping that the chick would leave by the end of the day, but she didn't. She listened when he told the hotel that she could order anything she wanted in his name, and he would pay. She had been ordering both things she needed and the things she didn't need because she knew that her client was equal to the task.

The guy received a call while at his place of work after one week and was told that this lady was still in the hotel and had incurred a whole lot of debt. The man was shocked to the marrow. He started plotting on how to ask her to leave. He called her, and she said that she was comfortable where she was and knew he could afford the bill. She used her sugar-coated mouth to brainwash this guy into asking him can she stay there till she was satisfied.

This chick stayed for more two weeks before she left the hotel because she found another client who offered better conditions. This dude's life was a mess. He didn't have enough money to pay the debt, and the hotel management kept coming after him.

This case is still going until today. This is the kind of case a bad bitch can serve you. It can be something similar or worse. Those people do not care to what extent they deal with you. Their comfort and their well-being comes first to them. They believe that they are the queens and all attention should be on them. Of course, the queen has to take care of her body to maintain the beauty.

Also, when this chick is done dealing with you or has found a better person, she will look for a means to take you out of her life. She can sleep with another dude to deal with you; usually it's someone of a higher class. She can employ thugs to deal with you or get you arrested. She can get people to kill you if you prove difficult. She will meet Mr. A today, suck the financial nutrients out of him, and move over to Mr. B. She is the "use and disappear" kind of lady. That chick will use you for the moment until you outgrow your usefulness, and then she would bullshit another dude. The cycle continues that way for her.

Once she meets you and is sure that you have money, her desire is to milk you of all your resources until there is none left. She will buy designers accessories, expensive weaves, exotic cars, and anything your money can buy.

Catching a disease. A bad bitch equals a hood rat in many ways. Like the hood rats, the bad bitch is a pack of diseases. Dealing with the hood rats is like playing with fire. It is worse in the bad bitch's case because she looks harmless and innocent. Do not think that because she is sexy and good looking, she will not have any diseases—this bitch is poison inside. Her beauty and elegance will deceive you into believing that she is without blemish, but this lady has been sleeping with a bunch of dudes and has contracted so many diseases in the process. She shares these diseases at will, giving them out as souvenirs.

A bad bitch is a bundle of issues packaged with a beautiful sheet. If it was one of the goods in a shop, customers would buy it first. But the problems that come with buying the item are beyond your comprehension.

Bell Biv DeVoe, in their song "Poison," expresses how dubious these chicks can be. I do not know about other people, but I believe they were referring to bad bitches. They advises, "Never to trust a big butt and a smile, that girl is poison." They stress that in some portions of the prisons, you will be comfortable, and "she is the best thing in the world." She is a scam that will "drive you out of your mind and steal your heartbeat while you are blind." She is a poison for real, and that poison works slowly and gets at you when you don't see it coming.

Whenever someone wants to give you poison, the person makes it presentable by putting in something attractive, something you would like when you see it. Because it looks good and attracts you, you are more likely to eat it. This is the same situation with this chick. She is a harmful substance coated with sugar.

You would be safer if you fucked this chick with protection, but in most cases, a situation will arise, and you won't mind fucking this chick without condoms. There are two situations that may lead to your contracting a disease or an infection from this chick.

1. The condom may break in the process of fucking this bitch, and you continue because you cannot deny yourself the pleasure of pulling out when you are already at your peak. You know that you are digging your grave in the process.

2. You may decide not to use a condom because this is a fine chick, and you want to hit it raw. You say, "This chick is so beautiful. Why would I use a condom to fuck her?" Then you do not use any protection.

It is easier to contract a disease from the bad chick than from the hood rat because of her enticing looks. You may be carried away by what you are seeing, and you are in a hurry to get there. You are not going to be as cautious as you would be when you see a hood rat. On seeing a hood rat, you may go get a condom if you do not have any, but at the sight of a bad bitch, you will not even remember that you need to protect yourself.

A bad bitch is a triple threat. She will drain your ass of your resources. She will also fuck around to break your ass. Remember that this chick has good physical features. You are proud to be with her, you can show her off to people because she is rare, and you would do anything to keep her. She will demand the impossible and you will be glad to get it for her. She will ask for a moon, and you will be outside the next day building a rocket. That's how crazy you can get trying to keep this chick who is out to deal with you.

You sit there and admire her beauty. You say, "Oh, my God! Is this woman really mine? I would be foolish to let this kind of woman pass me by."

Bad bitches come in a variety of shapes, sizes, and skin tones. Some are of the slender body, and others are a bit plump. The only thing is that no matter their shape, size, and skin tone, they always look stunning. No matter how different their shapes or sizes are, they have two things in common: their striking good looks and their gold-digging hustle. They use their sexyness and their status as a commodity to get the things they need. By commodity, I mean something people want to buy, something that is of value to people so that they want to own it. It is something that the owner can make money off of by renting it out. At the very least, the bad bitch knows that she is a meal ticket. She can make a demand, and dudes will struggle to be the one to meet the demand.

A chick like this will never be homeless. As a matter of fact, she has so many men offering to get her an apartment or to let her stay at his place.

Very few of these chicks get pregnant and give birth; it's due only to a failed relationship. Once in a while, a bad bitch can meet a guy who is so nice, and they fuck up. This dude has everything she wants in a man, and she will start plotting how to get more money from this dude. She may think if she becomes the guy's baby mama, she may get more than she is already getting from him. This is the one time she may use pregnancy as bait. She informs the guy that she is pregnant and expects to get money from him for her upkeep. This works for them most times, because the guy is very happy to have this beauty as the mother of his child. He will therefore do anything possible to have and keep a baby by this woman.

On the other hand, the bad bitch may meet a dude who is a baller or pretends to be a baller. This is the kind of guy she may want to keep when she is tired of fucking around, stripping, and setting up guys. She may think if she gets pregnant for him, she may have a chance of being his woman. She will fuck up and not take her birth control pills to get pregnant.

If she gets pregnant, she will take care of the child. Once she gives birth, which will happen only once, she will see to the child's welfare. She won't behave like the hood rat, who can give her child to anyone who cares to take it. The bad bitch will still use her good looks to get enough money to take care of the child. Providing for the child is not a problem because she has money and can always get more money from men. She has multiple choice of men. She can divide her needs and share them among a number of men at hand. Mr. A may pay for her apartment, Mr. B will see to her food, Mr. C will take care of what she wears, and so on. At any point in time, if she needs money, there must be someone to give her the amount she wants.

She will never allow herself to get pregnant again. It is difficult to see a bad bitch with two or three children. Having one child is very rare, let alone having so many children. Once she gives birth, she tells herself, "This is not the end of the world. I have to get back to the real me and continue my hustle." She hits the gym, and within months, she is back to her normal shape.

There was this chick in my hood. She packed in when she was pregnant. She was really gorgeous. News flew around that she was always seen in the clubs or hotels with men of affluence until she played the wrong game. She met this guy at the club after stripping for the night. Their connection at the first meeting was so strong that she felt the chemistry between them. She went to his house with him that night. After staying for the night, she stayed for a week. She was comfortable around him and thought about settling down with him.

The best trap she thought she could use for him was getting pregnant for him, and she did so. The result of the pregnancy wasn't what she foresaw. The dude gave her some money for her upkeep and asked her to leave his house. That was when she came to our neighborhood. Some months later, she delivered a baby boy.

A few weeks after she delivered, she made the gym her second home, and she fought to get back in shape. It worked for her. Now, this chick has totally transformed into something to be desired. She has hit the club again, though she no longer stays in the hood.

This is exactly what happens to the bad bitch if she ever miscalculates. She does not slouch, however. The bad bitch picks herself up and gets back on track; she never makes the same mistake again. Her body may not remain the same after the workouts and pills because a woman's body must undergo some changes after she gives birth. But some bad bitches get very close to getting it back. Regardless, they do not lose their beauty. They are still beautiful but are not quite as they used to be.

IMPLICATIONS OF HAVING A CHILD WITH A BAD BITCH

Having a child with this type of woman is an epic mistake. You may ask why considering your child would copy the mother's good looks. This chick monetizes every part of her life. To spent time with her, you must spend money. To smash this chick, you must spend money. To see her, you must spend money. In fact, anything that concerns her is expensive.

If maintaining this woman is this expensive, you can imagine what will happen if she has a baby for you. She will empty your wallet. She looks for reasons to ask for money. As a matter of fact, you become her bank, where she comes to withdraw money.

If these chicks ever gets pregnant, the father of the baby is usually a celebrity, a drug dealer, a baller, a singer, a rapper, a famous person, or a politician. A bad bitch cannot be pregnant for a cheap-ass driver. Once you hear that this kind of chick has a baby, know that the father of the baby is one of those people mentioned earlier. This tells you that she doesn't get pregnant for the sake of having a baby. It is a well-plotted plan.

If you make six figures and above, this kind of woman will likely run games on you. She is always out for people who makes a lot of money. You need to be extra careful about this chick.

Self-esteem. A bad bitch has high self-esteem. She has this confidence in herself because of obvious reasons. She has charm and a stunning figure. She is so proud of what she does, the number of men she meets, and the money she makes from this venture.

She doesn't go around the hood bragging because of the class she operates on, but she still tells stories of exploits with pride to her friends. She is the owner of the loud voice that tells her friends shit like, "He is proud because he hasn't seen a pretty woman like me."

A certain chick came back with her new ride, and her friends came around to celebrate with her. She told them that the gift came from one of her boyfriends. They hailed her, and her beauty gave her so much confidence. She believed she could attract anyone she chose with her body.

Ratchet level. This type of chick is very nasty. This is usually because she gets anything she wants. If you step on her toes, she knows men of higher authority whom she can call to deal with you. Do not get into any case with this chick. She will seduce the person presiding over the case and get him on her side.

Level of entitlement. This chick has an overinflated sense of entitlement. She feels like she is so pretty, and therefore things should happen in her favor.

Last week, I went to pick up my mom from the airport, and I saw a pretty chick of about twenty. She saw the traffic, and cars were coming, but she stepped into traffic. The traffic had to stop for her to pass.

This is how enormous her level of entitlement was. She thought every car should hold on for her to pass because she was so pretty. A bad bitch does this kind of thing. When she meets this dude who has money, she asks for money from him as if the dude makes money only for her. She feels that people should put her interests and needs first.

In this day and age, people treat you better because you are beautiful. You get what you want easily if you have a pretty face. You can jump a queue, and everyone will allow it because you look stunning, but an ugly person would not think of it. If an ugly girl tries this, I am sure a car would run over her and pretend that it didn't see her.

The bad bitch has been pretty her whole life, and getting favors from people has been easy for her. She doesn't know what it means for someone to turn her down. She therefore thinks that it would be difficult for someone to say no to her.

I have heard some ladies discussing the kind of treatment they receive from their men and the changes they would want to make in their relationships. One of those ladies was the loudest. She claimed that her boyfriend had a lot of money. She didn't know how rich he was, but she knew that the guy was rich enough to get her anything she wanted. She didn't want to know whether the guy had more to take care of himself or his family. She said, "I am not sure whether any member of his family is as beautiful as I am, so he needs to take care of this beautiful skin before he thinks of anything else. If he has to go hungry to do it, so be it." I immediately knew that she was a bad bitch. This chick wanted to the be the subject, and others would be objects.

Employment. A bad bitch cannot work in a cooperate establishment. Like the hood rat, she wouldn't even fit in. If she is employed, it would be as a stripper in the high-end strip clubs, or an escort. If she is lucky, she may get modeling jobs or become a video ho.

Bad bitches are usually those pretty chicks they use for the front page of books or magazines, or in music videos. I saw one chick used on the front cover of a magazine. One day I saw her and decided to talk to her and get her phone number because she was a fine. When I got to know her, I saw that she was a bad bitch, and I bailed.

WHAT MAKES A BAD BITCH DANGEROUS?

A bad bitch is a pack of problems. Once you welcome this kind of woman in your life, you have accepted problems.

1. **She is extremely deceptive and highly manipulative.** She has her way of benignly extorting money from men. You will be surprised if your mother or sister asks you for money, but if a bad chick asks for money, you would gladly forget your family for this chick. She knows how to manipulate her way into your heart, and you think that she loves and cares for you, but those things are drama. She wants only your wallet. Do not fall for her manipulative techniques.

If you know the way these chicks operate, it would be easier for you to resist them, but if you are naive, they will use you to achieve their selfish desires.

2. **Her looks will disarm you**. The way she looks instantly disarms you. You immediately start thinking with your dick. A bad chick has a charm; you'd find it difficult to see this chick without uttering, "This chick is gorgeous." Owing to the fact that she looks amazing, you stop thinking with your brain and want to smash her as soon as you can.

If you are reading this book and consider yourself a red pill man or a man of unwavering fortitude, or if you have uncompromising qualities, know that this kind of woman can be out to get you. Do not be surprised if you have to do away with all your endearing qualities to get to this woman. You may think that you can meet a bad bitch only in the hood. You say, "I can never meet this chick because I do not go to the hood to look for chicks." A bad chick is everywhere. You can meet her outside the hood, but she comes from the hood. She operates like a chick from the hood. She still possesses all those characters that a bad bitch is known for regardless of where you meet her. She has that gold-digging spirit.

3. **She has so many alternatives.** A bad bitch has a lot of people who want to roll with her, and she takes pride in it. She will turn down your requests because they do not meet her standards. She tells you stuff like, "I can't go out with you because the place you are taking me tonight is too cheap for my liking." She shows you what other guys have done for her so that you will step up your game. She hides nothing about her being with other guys from you. She tells you, "I can't go out with you this weekend because a certain guy is taking her to a certain place." She tells you that because she knows the guys she plans to go out with will offer more than what you can offer. But she does her calculations, and if she sees that she can gain more by going out with you, she won't cancel her appointment with you. It is as if the guys are taking numbers to see her, and they know it, but they are comfortable with it.

The funny thing about it is that the guys are blind enough to not notice she is playing games on them. She tells a guy that she may not go out with him and gives him one flimsy excuse. Then the guy says, "Do you mind fitting me in next weekend?" This is a red flag that this guy was supposed to watch out for, but he still walked right into the ditch.

This situation is real, and these chicks are real. They do not hide their attitude, not even on social media. You can go to Instagram and see many of them displaying what they are made of in their comments.

Class. Everything about this bitch looks good. She is a classy woman. She buys the best weave that look like her real hair. Everything she has is authentic. She buys and wears the best of jewelry, designer clothes and bags, the most expensive makeup, and the costliest shoes. She takes care of her body and would break her neck in the gym to ensure that she doesn't lose her beautiful shape. She goes to the best gym and has the best personal trainer. She has baby hairs. She has a specific diet to keep her body in shape. You see her doing morning workouts. She probably does Kegel exercises and practices sucking dick with some bananas. She probably attends dick-sucking classes. You may wonder whether there is anything like dick-sucking classes. Yes, these classes exist, and most times the chicks you see there are from this category.

The bad bitch takes care of herself so that it is difficult for you to guess her age. The chick looks younger than her age. This kind of chick could be thirty-five but will pass for a chick of twenty-five. Her face is like a china doll. She has the image of a perfect being. She is able to maintain this class because she makes money from her stripping job. She can go stripping for the night and come back with a lot of money. Dudes stand in line to spend money on her. She has so many guys waiting in line to pay her bills.

This chick is always on a vacation in the Bahamas, Dubai, and other good places, taking good pictures and uploading them on social media for people to see. You may wonder how she has the money to afford this kind of life. The money she is spending comes from guys she exploits. And the guys are happy that they are able to provide the woman with the kind of lifestyle she deserves without knowing that they have been caught in this woman's snare.

Some months ago, I went strolling with one of my friends. We hoped to check out the chicks in the hood and talk to some of them. We saw different types of women, but one particular chick with a stunning look caught our attention. I approached this lady and talked to her for a few minutes. It didn't take me long to know the kind of woman she was, and I fled for my life. My friend remained relentless and said he loved her despite all my warnings. Soon, this chick moved in with him, and now she goes on vacation to any country of her choice. My friend actually brags about it; he feels he is a real man who has been able to give his woman everything she wants.

You can tell from this story that my guy does not even know what he is doing. I am tempted to say that his brain is no longer functioning. In place of his brain, his dick is doing the thinking. It is not only with this guy—the same thing is happening to other dudes who are rolling with this type of women. Their desire is to give her the most ravishing lifestyle they can think of, just to keep their women. These dudes can kill themselves spending everything that they have so that they can give her anything she demands from them in order to keep her from leaving their sides. If you found out how much guys spend to keep this bitch, you wouldn't believe it. You may even look at the guy and say that he is not the kind of guy who should be going out with this kind of chick based on his looks or anything else, but he has money, and that is what the chick is interested in.

Attractiveness. This chick is extremely attractive. No matter the shape and size she appears as, she is always a beauty to behold. This is the chick who has been told that she is pretty her whole life.

Intelligence level. The bad bitch is very intelligent. She knows how beautiful she looks, and she capitalizes on it. It takes a person who is very intelligent to do that. There are some bitches who are quite pretty but do not capitalize on their looks. They fuck every Tom, Dick, and Harry for free. This chick wouldn't try that shit. She works for her money, and she gets it.

Ambition level. Her ambition level is very high. She will not go for anything below the best. She goes out only with men of the high class. She goes for the best outfits, makeup, and shoes. She aims high and knows that there are some men who will give her exactly what she wants.

Traditional. This kind of chick is not traditional at all. She doesn't cook or clean for anybody. Those things are below her standards, and she wouldn't consider doing them at all. If she gets into a relationship with men, she prefers to get a maid to take care of the house and do the cleaning and the cooking. Her job is to check how well the maid has prepared a meal and how clean the house is, but her major job is to sit around and look pretty. She will tell you that she gets paid to look pretty, so why would she mess up her beauty by doing chores? It would change her color or break her nails.

A bad bitch is not one of those chicks who work nine to five. She takes care of her body. She won't indulge in anything that would stress her.

Let me remind you once more that I am not saying that all pretty chicks in the hood are bad bitches, but these qualities differentiate bad bitches from the other pretty chicks. There are other chicks in the hood who are as pretty as the bad bitches but live regular lives because they do not want to objectify themselves. I have been in contact with some of them, and they would do a regular jobs; they wouldn't strip or do anything that has to do with prostitution because they have respect for themselves.

Hustle. This chick is a hustler. Her hustling spirit is unmatched. She strives to make money and doesn't mind the means. The objective is to get money from men, and she is usually successful.

Ratchet level. This chick is very nasty and has a lot of attitude. Certain circumstances make her mellow so that she gets what she wants from guys. She may have to play a submissive role when she is in a relationship with guys who have money.

Marriage. It is very possible for this type of chick to be in a long-term relationship or get married. As long as you have the money to take care of her, she is willing to submit to you—at least until she finds another person who can give her more than you are bringing to the table. Sometimes these men who have bad bitches as girlfriends may not want to lose them forever, and they therefore make them their wives.

Traditional type. If we were not in an era when whoring culture was popularized, this kind of chick would be called a trophy wife.

She demands money for all sorts of things so she can look pretty, and you meet her demands so she doesn't leave. She won't do anything at home except look after her body. She operates exactly the same way she operates now. The only difference is that it wouldn't be as glorified as it is now. Bitches and gold diggers have always existed.

WHO IS HER MATCH?

Research has proven that it pays to be beautiful. People do things to your favor if you are beautiful. This chick has been beautiful since she was small, and that is how she has been getting attention and favors her whole life. She believes that the world revolves around her and she gets anything as soon as she asks for it.

A bad bitch believes in "I get what I ask for." She thinks all dudes are gullible and can easily be enticed by her charm. She thinks that she is beautiful, and therefore everything and anything she asks for should be given to her. She may not have met anybody who has told her no. If she ever meets a dude who would look straight into her eyes and say no to her requests, she would think he was the craziest dude on the planet. That guy is the perfect match for her.

This is how players use this kind of woman without spending a dime. The players create a mental picture of how fat their bank accounts are through word of mouth and his fake lifestyle. The bitch may think that she will be able to change him to spend his money on her by hanging on for a while. The guy will decline her requests while saving his money from being wasted.

This kind of chick used to be in a relationship where she dictated the pace—what happened and when. She said when you go on vacation, when you have sex with her, and even when you eat out. She is used to lording over the men and having them obey her commands. If you prove to defy her charm by being disciplined and saying no to her requests, you have won her heart forever. But you must have something that she wants: you must have a character that will endear her to you. It may be the way you speak to her or something unique about you that she doesn't see in any random guy she meets.

RELATIONSHIP BETWEEN THE HOOD RAT AND THE BAD BITCH

The bad bitch is the counterpart of the hood rat. Better put, the bad bitch is the rival of the hood rat. At the end of the day, the hood rat gets the crumbs of what the bad bitch has taken. The hood rats get the leftovers when the bad bitch has made her choices. Let's say about ten men come around the hood to check out the chicks. The first type of chick they see and develop interest in is the bad bitch. If all of them talk to the chicks, they pick those that are fancy—maybe about four of them or more. The rest want to talk to another chick. The next kind of chick they are likely to meet is the hood rat. That is exactly what I mean by leftover. If the bad bitch didn't exist, these men would head straight for the hood rats, but the presence of the bad bitch has obstructed this direct contact, thereby making the bad bitches their rivals.

A hood rat and a bad bitch are involved in the same profession. But whereas a bad bitch does only stripping and prostitution, a hood rat does other jobs such as doing and selling drugs. The only reason a hood rat does this multitasking is because she does not make enough money from her stripping and prostitution business; she does not look as adorable as a bad bitch, so she has to steal or set up some niggas to be robbed.

The bad bitch can charge whatever she wants because of her class and her looks, and she gets paid. The hood rat is already dealing with people of the lower classes. She knows that she cannot tell them what to pay. She instead collects the little she can get from and backs it up with side hustles.

Whereas the hood rat is seen at the strippers' place, clubhouses, and motels on the lower end, the bad bitch visits hotels with class and other recreational places. She is able to afford those places because of the class of people she attracts.

A hood rat and a bad bitch are on two ends of a parallel line; they are almost the same features but operate at different levels. The hood rat is at the low end, and the bad bitch is at the high end. If a hood rat was beautiful like the bad bitch, she would operate exactly the way the bad bitch does.

The bad bitch, like the hood rat, brags about her line of business and how good she is in bed, but she does not make it as loud as the hood rat makes it. She has her own selected friends with whom she discusses her business. This makes her lifestyle classy. The hood rat goes about the hood making noise of the shameful acts she engages in. The bad bitch blows her trumpet only within her enclosed circle.

WHY SHOULD YOU AVOID A BAD BITCH?

You do not need to avoid a bad bitch because she looks good. You need to avoid her because of the way she operates. You need to avoid this chick because of her mentality. She believes she is pretty and should be paid for being beautiful. She wants to be paid for everything. The only way a dude can spend some time with her or get her attention is with money. She thinks, "I am a pretty chick. You are gonna pay me for talking to you, pay for taking my contact, pay me for going out on a date with you, and pay me for knowing my name." Everything about her is about money.

These guys are her means of making money for herself. Being in a relationship with this chick means making yourself one of her money-making machines. Only when she knows that she can get money from you does she allow you to talk with her in the first place. If you have no money, then you do not have business with her.

When she finally decides whom she really wants to settle down with, it is going to be a regular dude who does not have a load of money. She can make this decision only after she hits the wall. You will be shocked to see the guy she falls in love with: he does not have money. This is why she is not the smartest chick on the list. All she does is live an expensive and ravishing lifestyle while she is young. When she is tired of stripping and whoring and decides to settle down, she settle for less. Once she hits the wall and her body starts telling her that old age is inevitable—the breasts start sagging and wrinkles start popping up—she goes for a regular dude who is not so rich.

CHAPTER 5

THE EDUCATED RATCHET

This is the worst type of chick on the list. She is the most dangerous of the five of them. This chick will destroy your life completely, and you will never see it coming. I bet you don't know how dangerous she is. You would never think that this chick is out to get you. This chick is different from the other types of chick. A thot can be classified as a ho. A mammy is not really a ho but can be one. A hood rat is a ho. A bad bitch is obviously a ho. But an educated ratchet is not a ho.

Educated ratchets are not as common as thots or mammies. On the other hand, they are not as rare as hood rats or bad bitches. They are somewhere in between. This type of chick is the most dangerous of all the chick types because they are a combination of all the qualities of those chicks. A mixture of a thot, mammy, hood rat, and bad bitch gives you an educated ratchet. The fact that they are all these chicks in one does not make them dangerous. What makes them worse than all the other chicks is their ability to hide those qualities.

They are gifted in hiding the real stuff they are made of. You would even vouch for them that they have never lied. These chicks are very cunning and tuck in all their bad attitudes into an innocent look. You may be unable to judge their personality at the surface level.

This chick appears to be beautiful, educated, intelligent, traditional, and any other good quality. Once you look at her, the first part of her you see is that beautiful part of her that would make you come for her. But when you come closer to her, you know that she is like window dressing.

THE EDUCATED RATCHET AND OTHER CHICKS IN THE HOOD

This type of woman is unique. She possesses all the other chicks' strength but not one of their weaknesses. She has all the good qualities of thots, mammies, hood rats, and bad bitches but doesn't have their bad traits. She can be referred to as the infinity ratchet.

- **The Educated Ratchet and the Thot**

She has a slender body like the thot, but she doesn't have her lousy behavior and doesn't wear too much makeup. She maintains a nude and even makeup. She doesn't dress like thots. She wears outfits that fit her stature.

Unlike the thot, she is not promiscuous and is never seen fucking a man in public places. She attaches value to herself and can maintain a long relationship. She does not sleep with any man available; she makes her choice and ensures that the man is able to take care of her needs. Instead of fucking men in public places, she hides where no eye will see her.

An educated ratchet can have children like a thot and take care of them. Whereas a thot is uneducated, an educated ratchet is highly educated.

Both types of women can be employed in an organization. The only difference is that a thot is employed at the low end, and the educated ratchet is employed at the high end.

The thot is satisfied with her present state and does not want anything that would bring change to her present situation. The educated ratchet is never satisfied. She wants to become better. She is ambitious and wants to grow by the day. She does not want the kind of life where she would enjoy today and suffer tomorrow. She would rather sit today and plan for the rainy days.

- **The Educated Ratchet and the Mammy**

She is career driven like the mammy. She is educated and would strive to get jobs in corporate establishments with her certificate. She won't relax once she gets this job and will work toward getting promoted to a better position. That is exactly what the mammy does. They both keep fighting to get better.

Unlike the mammy, she maintains her pretty figure. She doesn't look large in size. This chick is the type you would see in the gym working out. She is the chick you would see jogging down the street on a daily basis because she doesn't want to look big. It is very rare to see a black woman jogging down the street, so if you do see one, it must be an educated ratchet. You see her jogging with enthusiasm, looking good in the ponytail she has, with a little bit of perspiration on her face. She wears tight-fitting running clothes and Nike Air Max. Also, she doesn't wear inappropriate dresses like a mammy. She has a good dress sense and knows which dress fits a particular occasion.

The mammy is not treated as a trophy wife. She gets everything she needs in her home by hustling for it. She provides for her children by doing her nine-to-five job. The educated ratchet gets some money from her husband. She works and gets paid, but the money belongs to her. The man she is in a relationship with is expected to cater to her needs.

For the educated ratchet, the formula is "Your money is ours, and my money is mine."

- **The Educated Ratchet and the Hood Rat**

She takes pride in everything she does, just like the hood rat. The only difference is that unlike the hood rat, she does not engage in any shameful activity. The hood rat takes delight in the fact that she sleeps around with men and gets some money from them in return. An educated ratchet would not indulge in such an act. She would rather take pride in her achievements, such as her newly acquired certificate or job promotion.

If for any reason an educated chick engages in a shameful act, she doesn't make it open for people to know. She doesn't let anyone hear it. She never lets it get to the ears of her sisters in her sorority. She would never let anybody catch her in a compromising position. She would never let people know her for a negative trait. If she ever wants to do anything bad, she does it in a place that is far from the eyes of the public, behind closed doors.

- **The Educated Ratchet and the Bad Bitch**

Just like the bad bitch, this chick knows her value, and she is relentless in getting whatever she deserves. She would never accept anything below her standards. If she sets her target, she never accepts defeat until she has met that goal. An educated ratchet knows her worth and never compromises.

An educated ratchet is just as pretty as the bad bitch. She knows how attractive she looks and therefore monetizes everything about herself, as the bad bitch does. She can afford expensive weaves and good clothes. She is classy. Unlike the bad bitch, the educated ratchet considers the long term before implementing her plans. This educated ratchet does not want to enjoy today and go bankrupt tomorrow. She would rather wait for that tomorrow when she can have everything in abundance.

The bad bitch meets different dudes with lots of cash, but when she hits the wall, she follows an average guy. In the case of the educated ratchet, she will stay with a guy for as long as possible, and whenever she feels like it, she will set up the dude, and everything that belongs to the guy will become hers. This is regardless of of age.

An educated ratchet is smarter than a bad bitch. She gets what she knows will last her a lifetime, whereas the bad bitch gets only what will take her a while until her beauty lasts.

FEATURES OF AN EDUCATED RATCHET

An educated ratchet is a beautiful chick who has a job to herself. This does not mean that all the ladies who work nine to five are educated ratchets. So many attributes come together to form the educated ratchet. This lady is cunning, driven, patient, disciplined, and vindictive.

- **Cunning.** Everything this chick does is part of her plan. Nothing ever happens by accident. She draws her plans, and they always fall in place. She has been planning this since she was a kid. She enrolled in school, made good grades and graduated high school, went to the college, joined a sorority, and made all her connections. If you ever meet this kind of lady, never think that she does anything because she loves you. Everything she does is for herself.

A chick was so beautiful that two men asked her out at the same time. These dudes knew that both of them were hitting on one girl, but neither would let go because of how beautiful this chick was. They agreed that if the chick chose either of them, the other should give up. The chick went for the first guy, and the second guy surrendered.

While she was with the first guy, she observed the second guy. When she finally concluded that the second guy had more money than the first one, she defected. She went to the second guy and told him how she'd loved him from the start, but the other guy wouldn't let her be. He tried convincing her by telling her how bad of a person he was. The second guy believed her cock-and-bull story and took her in. The guy went to the extent of confronting the first guy, and the rest was history.

This is the kind of woman who will tell you lies that can make best friends become enemies. Before this chick takes any step, she does lots of calculations to ensure that she is the one to benefit.

- **Driven.** This chick is purpose-driven. She knows what she wants and is willing to do anything to get to the point she envisions. She is not deterred at any point. She has a dream and does everything possible to live up to that dream. This is the same spirit she has that makes her deal with you if you step on her toes.

- **Patient.** The educated ratchet is not in a hurry to see her results. She has planted her seeds and is sure that they will grow. She has set her priorities and pressed the right keys, and she will stay by the side and watch everything mature. She wants to get to the peak of her career, and she will pick up the right attitude, talk to the right set of people, and expect that with time she will get promotions.

This is that type of chick who is willing to wait for your huge amount of money to mature. I have heard stories of chicks who stood by their boyfriends when they were managing, until the guy made money or inherited a whole lot of money.

She is willing to wait. She is ready to play the long game. She doesn't have to be a stripper or a prostitute because of her good looks. She knows that the kind of money she could make from that business is short-term money. It is not the kind of money that would last. It is only the kind of money that would be available as long as she had her good looks.

Once she hit the wall and everything sagged, that would be the end to her stripping money.

She does long-term planning and gets ready for the period when she won't look this pretty anymore. She sets her retirement plan. She will wait for that big money.

- **Disciplined.** This chick has her principles. There are so many things she would do, and there are others that she wouldn't try. This is the type of chick who wouldn't allow you to sleep with her upon the first meeting. If you are a kind of dude for which she has no value, she can give you pussy on the first night. She can allow you if she simply wants to have fun or wants to validate herself. You are her plaything, and you won't even notice that she is using you. You have no idea that you are a walking dildo. But if you are the dude that she has carved out to be her mark, and if you are her ideal man and the type she wants to have in her life, she will never let you sleep with her the first time you meet. The one she has sex with at the first meeting is her toy, whereas the other guy she marks is her retirement plan.

- **Vindictive.** This chick has a tendency to seek revenge if you wrong her. She does not forgive easily. If you ever cross her, she will crush you. She won't wait for you to push her to the wall before she reacts. Once you push her, she strikes back. She doesn't care how long you have known her, how long you have been dating, or how long you have been married.

I read a biography of a young woman who planned her life from childhood. She had her college degree and was employed in one of the biggest companies in the state. She met a man whom she fell in love with at the young age of fifteen. She was still young and naïve. This guy deflowered her and introduced her to the world of sexuality. She trusted him and gave him every part of her. She didn't go to stay with him, but they saw each other every day. At the age of seventeen, she got pregnant with this guy baby. She told him about the pregnancy, and the guy pretended to be happy with the development.

One day, the dude got her a drink, and she took it, not knowing that it contained abortion-inducing drugs. Moments later, she felt sharp pains followed by bleeding. That was how she lost her baby. She found out later that it was her boyfriend who killed her baby, but she couldn't do anything because the dude was from a rich background.

Years later, she grew up into a very attractive and well-educated lady. Their paths crossed again, and he hit on her again. She accepted him once more and forgave him. At that time, this dude was already earning up to six figures and had so many investments. They dated for three years and got married. She had two kids by him. This dude had been relaxed because he had gotten everything he wanted in life. Then this lady struck.

She gave herself several injuries with her kitchen knife and called the cops. The dude was arrested and was taken to court. After several sittings, the guy lost the case and was asked to pay for damages.

An educated ratchet never forgives. She may not strike back immediately; she may wait for a time when she has enough resources and other weapons to fight back. She will take up your case and follow it religiously until she is sure you are doomed. This chick will not just set you up—she will legally take everything you have worked for and make them her own. But this is not her being vindictive; it is simply her pattern of operation.

Physical features. This chick is very beautiful. She is slim like the thot but does not wear funny makeup, and she doesn't dress inappropriately. She wears makeup that is perfect with her skin and outfit. She has a killer smile that can charm you the first time you meet her. She always looks happy whenever you see her. Someone was trying to describe an educated ratchet he met, and he said that the chick was smiling at him at the party as if they had met before.

This chick has some baby hairs. She will pull her hair back, and with the comb, she will define the baby hairs so that they can be easily seen by applying some oil on them and making a wavy look.

She always wears good weaves. She can afford the expensive weaves, nice articles of clothing that blend with her stature, and other accessories to complement her looks.

Activities. An educated ratchet is highly educated and smart. She can sleep with men and get paid for her services, but they hide it from people so that if her secret ever leaked, people would never believe it. She is that classy working chick who can sleep with a man in a hotel room, wake up very early the next day, dress up for work with her blended makeup, and head straight to the office.

This type of chick knows so many things, especially things that have to do with women and their education. She has read many books about feminism and what they stand for. She can hit you with arguments on topics that concern feminism. She is the kind of woman who would come to you with the "I am a woman; hear me roar" attitude. She will not do anything in the house that reduces her standards, such as cleaning, ironing, cooking, or doing dishes. Those chores can be done by anybody. If the only person available to do it is the guy, she sees nothing wrong with it.

Like the hood rat, this chick can be extremely manic, volatile, and physically violent. This chick can get physical with anyone who steps on her toes. You need to be careful with this chick. Though she has a pretty look, if you push her to the wall, she may take a swing at you, and you will be surprised at the outcome. The crazy part is that she is a professional at hiding all these characters and tendencies.

A man was unlucky enough to get into a heated argument with this kind of chick. The argument came to a point where the chick wanted it to end, but the dude wouldn't let go. She punched the guy in the face and waited for his reaction. In annoyance, he gave her a slap. She went into the bathroom and slapped the hell out of her face so that it became swollen. She picked up a phone and called the cops. When the cops came, she cooked up a credible story of how the dude had assaulted her. The cops believed every word that came from her mouth and arrested the dude.

The cops looked only at her beauty and believed that such a pretty face could not lie. She seemed like such an innocent woman. She was not a stripper like the bad bitch. She was not a prostitute like the hood rat. She was in the good books of many people, so she couldn't cook up such lies.

An educated ratchet is not seen as a ho like the other women. She has a regular day job, leaves the house in the morning, and comes back in the evening. She has a good paying job and has gotten her degree. She doesn't stay in the slums and has a very decent apartment for herself in the suburbs.

This chick will get you in trouble and feel no remorse for what she has done. She can come up with something that looks like the truth to get your ass put in jail, and she will be unapologetic about it. She can show up in court if it gets to that point. You will see her in court crying her eyes out, and you can't help but declare her innocent. She puts up an act that will surprise you. She says, "I was just so afraid. I thought he was going to kill me. I didn't know I was going to make it." This chick is deadly.

This is the black chick who puts realism into her act. She does exactly the same thing that white women do. She plays on the sympathies of the patriarchy, and she is willing to use the entire system to her advantage.

This chick gets involved in shameful acts, but she is an expert at hiding her naughty behaviors. She wouldn't let her sisters, neighbors, or society to find out what she is doing or what she has done. She allows people to see only the beautiful and perfect part of her. This kind of woman brings you to ruin faster than a thot. A thot wouldn't take it this far. This bitch is heartless and will be happy to see to your downfall if she wants to get you down. If she is on your case, she will follow it up and make sure that you end up in prison.

An educated ratchet knows that she has a beautiful set of eyes, a pretty face, and a charming smile. She capitalizes on this, coupled with her level of education and her status as a commodity, to monetize every aspect of her.

QUALITIES THAT EDUCATED RATCHETS LOOK FOR IN THEIR MEN

If you get into a relationship with this chick, you will see that everything about her is money. She gives you excuses with how busy she is or how tight her schedule is, but if you are going to drop some money for her, you see that she is available for you. She only accepts going on dates to exotic hotels where the bills for a lunch would equal a year's rent.

This implies that for you to be in a relationship with this chick, you must meet some qualifications.

1. You must be rich.
2. You must have a college education.
3. You must be a baller.

1. **You must be rich.** For this woman to accept being in a relationship with you, she must make sure that you are a rich guy or come from a rich family. This chick has no business with a poor guy. Once she sees you, she checks whether your pocket is heavy enough to take care of her needs. So many men want to be in a relationship with this chick because of how she carries herself and her beauty. She is smart enough to know the difference between a guy who is really rich and a guy who pretends to be rich.

2. **You must have a college education.** This chick has a standard already and has her college degree. She doesn't operate below that standard. She is picky when it has to do with friends, and her picky attitude has a role to play when men flock around her. An educated ratchet is educated and believes that she should roll only with people of her class—people who have the same degree as her or a higher degree. A guy who has no college education is below her standards and is unworthy to be with her.

3. **You must be a baller.** An educated ratchet seeks not just a rich guy but a baller. You must be able to spend the money. If she is in a relationship with you, you should be able to earn six figures, drive a nice car, take her on vacations, and get her a nice house. Even if you have all the money in the world, if you do not have the spirit to spend it, she will never come near you. This kind of woman will tell you, "I don't want to know that you earn six figures—I want to see you spend the fucking money." For this chick, the money you spend is directly proportional to the love she has for you.

EXPECTATIONS OF AN EDUCATED RATCHET

If you are unlucky to be in a relationship with this chick, know that she has a lot of expectations of you. She expects that you know what her problems are, and you should solve them even before she brings them to you. She wants you to see her as a queen and make sure she lacks for nothing. She knows you have the money and does not want to hear that you cannot afford something she demands.

This lady makes a lot of demands of men who are in relationships with her. The only difference is that she does it with tact. She has a way of making you spend lots of money on her without knowing it. You won't even know how much you have spent on her. She keeps asking for more, and at the end of the day, she will ask you to marry her. If she doesn't ask you, she expects that you should ask her to marry you.

She expects you to be her Prince Charming. Propose to her with the most expensive diamond ring while saying many beautiful words to her. Plan the most expensive wedding and give her a home of her dreams. Her entitlement level has no restrictions.

She has a mental picture of an engagement party that will be held on a ship or at an expensive spot—the type that would be featured in weekly magazines. You fall short of her expectations if you do not meet those standards.

WHAT MAKES THIS CHICK MANIC AND VOLATILE?

The educated ratchets show tendencies of being manic and volatile. They get easily irritated around people who are below their standards. They cannot stand the beggars. At the same time, they can easily get angry at things. A single comment made by a colleague at work can change their mood for the rest of the day. They may not be aware that they are acting inappropriately. The following signs show the manic nature in them.

- She shows aggression if anyone challenges her views. These type of chick does not need opposition. She wants her ideas or suggestions to override any others. She intentionally brings her suggestions when the agenda is about to be concluded. She gets aggressive if her options are not considered.

You do not need to give her your opinion about her behavior. This chick does not stand to be corrected; she is right in everything she does. She may attack you if you try voicing your opinion or telling her she is wrong. Once you challenge her, you become her enemy.

- She sees herself as being more important and having more connections than other people. She believes that she knows people at the high end. She never believes any other person is more connected than she is. If you fuck up with her, she knows the number she can dial to put you in jail. If she needs anything, she knows whom to call. The fact that she knows these people makes her very important. This chick doesn't mind if the occupants of the neighborhood prostrate for her to walk on them.

- She sometimes engages in unusual behavior such as extravagant spending, unwise consumption of alcohol, and reckless sex. This chick occasionally gets the kind of men who are ready to spend their money. The educated ratchet will assist the men in wasting their resources at expensive clubs and hotels. Sometimes she wants to have fun. She engages in excessive alcoholic consumption and reckless sexual behavior. This is the moment she meets those men she wants to have fun with, and she takes them as dildos. She does not want anything from them except good sex. She uses those men to her advantage. She engages in these acts and sweeps it under the carpet so that prying eyes will not see it.

- She has overconfidence in her abilities. She believes that no one can do it better than she can. In her relationships, she believes that no one will be a better girlfriend or wife than her. In her workplace, she sees herself as indispensable. She thinks no one will be able to carry out her duties the way she does. Even in the social world, she believes she knows it all. This is part of the reasons that she doesn't want correction from anyone.

Intelligence level. This kind of chick is highly intelligent. It takes a very smart woman to operate in this way. In her dealings, she is careful to not expose the part of her that she has kept in the cupboard so that the eyes of the public will not see it. She is the smartest type in this book. She plans her life well and makes sure it favors her at the end of the day.

She goes through school to get a formal education. She is able to secure a job for herself and get handsomely paid. She gets a rich guy and tries to settle with him. The guy may marry her, or she will go and stay with him, but there are greater chances that she will be a wife. While staying with the guy, she may or may not bear children for him. When the time is right, she will set up the guy and make away with the dude's children and all he has worked to achieve.

This is a perfect plan. Everything that happens in her life revolves around this cycle. In the long run, she enjoys the most luxurious lifestyle among the chicks in the list when they retire. The bad bitch would enjoy this too, but she makes only short-term plans. She doesn't consider what happens to her when she loses her beauty; she simply enjoys it while it lasts. The educated ratchet is smart enough to consider her tomorrow and exercise the patience to get it.

As far as her gold-digging skill is concerned, she makes the bad bitch look like an amateur. You know the power that the bad bitch wields when it comes to gold digging? She is still learning compared to the educated ratchet. A bad bitch can become a video vixen. She can get a kingpin, dope boy, rapper, or movie star. But the educated ratchet can attract a corporate master of the universe. She can attract those people who are seen as masters of wealth because she is driven, disciplined, and smart enough to do it.

Do not get this twisted. It is not all of them who go in this direction. Some of them play around too much and wouldn't know when age starts setting in. They may forget that a time will come when their beauty fades. The smart ones are able to do all the scheming and conniving in their twenties; they get a dude they want and start working on him early enough. They have this dude in the background while they go about their secret thot behavior that no one knows about. They have this guy at home, and they also have their playthings and walking dildos.

Employment: This chick is educated and has her college degree. She is able to get jobs with her certificate. She usually gets regular paying jobs and is the kind of chick who can work nine to five. She is hardworking and industrious, especially when it comes to her work. She dutifully carries out her responsibilities in her workplace. She is the kind of chick who comes in as a new staff, and soon everyone in the organization knows her because of her outstanding performance.

I knew an educated ratchet that I used to work with; She used to stay in our hood sometime ago. I knew her as a hood chick, but I didn't know she was this good at what she did. She was recruited as an office assistant. Not long after that, she started winning "staff of the week." It was a shock to everyone because no one has ever gotten the award consecutively, but she carried the award week after week. This attracted the owner of our company, and the board made her the head of a department.

This chick wasn't bribing the management team. She simply found a way to efficiently carry out her tasks. She was punctual to the office and delivered the tasks given to her before the deadline. If she had to make presentation, she delivered it with ease. This positive attitude she brought to work made it easy for her to earn promotions. It did not take her long to climb the ladder of her career. An educated ratchet is good at what she does. This kind of woman always works in corporate America.

Self-esteem. An educated ratchet has high self-esteem. She has confidence that she can get anything she sets her mind to achieve. This chick is very proud of herself and her achievements. The bad bitch has only good figures and self-confidence that is pronounced, even in her speech. You can imagine the kind of self-worth an educated ratchet can have. She is very pretty and well educated with a good-paying job. This chick does not know the definition of low self-esteem. She carries herself as if she is the only woman in the world.

She chooses her circle and doesn't identify with everybody in the hood. It must be someone who is pretty, has money, or is educated. If you have none of these qualities, she will make sure your paths never cross.

This kind of chick cannot be easily manipulated. No matter how close you are to her or how she bonds with you, she will never allow you to manipulate her, no matter the technique you use. She knows how to be assertive and how best to handle different situations with a different attitude.

Submissiveness. This type of chick thinks so highly of herself. Her self-worth, education, and employment status make her less submissive and less a homemaker. She is not as submissive as other women because she believes that she has attained some level of achievement. Being submissive to a man becomes difficult. She therefore cannot be a homemaker.

She believes in feminism and preaches it. She sees no reason why she would be the one to cook, clean, and do all the chores. She believes that if she submits to you, she is serving you, and she never wants a situation where she serves anybody. She would rather be served. She says, "No man is below the other. I give you what you give me in the relationship. If you give me coffee, I will prepare a coffee for you."

This kind of chick does not stand for being controlled. She wants to own her life. To her, a man is only a part of her life. She wouldn't let a man order her about, telling her what to do and what not to do, where she can go and where she cannot go, what to say and what she cannot say, what she can put on and what she cannot put on, whom to relate with and whom not to relate with. She wants to be in charge of her life—and in charge of yours, if she can.

Ambition level. An educated ratchet is career driven. She is educated and usually gets jobs. When she is employed in these firms, she does not remain in a particular position for long. She grows and tries to be better than she was. The educated ratchet usually gets promotions because of her zeal and hard work. This type of chick can be employed in an organization today, and in one year, you wouldn't believe the position she holds in that same organization because she has worked so hard for it.

She is always on the go to hit the big bucks because she must incorporate it in her retirement plan. She aims high and allows only rich men in her circles. This chick does not believe that she can be on the low end or remain there for long. She employs all the distinctive features, she has to get the best life for herself.

Class level. This woman is classy. She doesn't overdo her makeup or clothes in a manner that she is the first person you notice in a gathering. She wears an outfit that flatters her shape. She does not make lots of noise, but her suggestions are very important in the meetings. She has so many ideas and suggestions. Once she stands up to talk in meetings, everyone wants to hear her because she is believed to be experienced.

Aside from dressing, being classy is seen all around her. Her taste is seen in the furniture in her room, the car she drives, and the plants around her.

Hustle. This chick is a hustler. Her kind of hustle is not like the thot or the hood rat because she has a college education. It is easier to get good jobs with good pay, but she doesn't rely on this. She puts in extra effort to move higher and earn higher. She brings home her hustling spirit. She scouts for money from her men and won't take no for an answer. She also takes care of her children from the money she makes from these men.

Ratchet level. This bitch is crazy and has a nasty attitude. She is crazy because of the level of entitlement she has, and this stems from the fact that she is pretty. When you are a beautiful woman in the hood, there is a level of entitlement you have because everyone kisses your ass. Everyone kissing her ass leads to a whole new level of narcissism.

Marriage. This chick usually gets married. Marriage is their ticket to make more money; it is the only way they can secure the money bag. Most times when she marks a man, she ensures that the dude marries her. She may not verbally ask the man to marry her, but she puts up an act. She seems like the type of woman you want to keep in the house as a wife. If she is out to get you to marry her, she plays her cards well by being so traditional that she cooks and cleans for you. You say, "Oh, my God, this woman is the complete package. She is beautiful and traditional as well. I am going to make her my wife." You do not know that it is a trap. She will deal with you if you fall into that ditch.

She also has the ability to stay in a long-term relationship. She only has problems with you when you do not provide for her as you used to, or if you try to order her around. If you are used to giving her a thousand bucks in a day, and you reduce it by one dollar, you are bound to lose her. She wants you to maintain a particular standard to take care of her. With an educated ratchet, it is always forward and never backward.

Remember that she is full of herself and will submit to no man, not even her husband. She has expectations that the guy will meet her as her husband. If he fucks up, she will divorce him immediately. If she has kids by you and divorces you, she will make sure she gets all the money, child support, your share of possessions, the car, and the house. She will get everything and will fight with the last drop of her blood to ensure it.

Children. This kind of chick can have zero to five children. She has zero before she gets married and up to five when she is married. The amount of children is dependent on the amount of money the man makes. The more the money he makes, the more the children she bears. If he is a multimillionaire, they will have up to five kids.

She is not into stripping or the whoring business, so she can actually have children and take care of them. She has enough money to see to the welfare of the children. In fact, her retirement plan covers herself and her children.

The fact that she has given birth does not mean she does not take care of herself. Upon giving birth, she hits the gym and continues her workouts. She is able to maintain her figure even after childbearing. This is the kind of chick who will keep her figure tight even after having five children. She is that sweet mom of five who will upload stunning pictures on the social media.

Traditional. An educated ratchet is traditional. This chick knows how to take care of the home and do the cooking and the cleaning, but she will never follow orders. She knows how to prepare a very delicious meal, but once you make it an order, then you have pressed the wrong button. She will show you the stuff she is made of and doesn't like to be ordered around. She prefers a situation where she is the one giving the orders.

Me and a friend of mine in my hood went to see a mutual friend. When we entered his house, I noticed a piece of paper pasted on the wall. Out of curiosity, I went closer to read it. I discovered that it was a duty roster that contained who did what and when. I had never seen such a thing before, and I showed my friend I came with the piece of paper. He wasn't surprised and told me the wife swore that she was not going to be a maid who served the man. They shared all the house chores between them and had some days of the week when they carried out their duties.

It is only an educated ratchet who can do this. She doesn't want to be under anybody control. She may willingly do the work, but once she perceives that she is serving you in any means, she retraces her steps. She would rather share the work with you: you may do the cleaning while she does the cooking, or vice versa.

Level of entitlement. This chick has an overinflated sense of importance. She feels like she deserves the world. It is possible that you can give the whole world and you not be with her. She believes that she should get some credit because of her reputation. This chick isn't as insane as the bad bitch by walking right into traffic, but she wonders why the traffic won't stop for her.

This chick's entitlement level is off the charts. In fact, she takes it that everything you own is hers, and everything she owns is just hers. You have nothing. She sees you as multipurpose. You are in her life to serve her. You are simply a figure in her life that is there to facilitate the things she wants. If she needs to shop, she can spend your money the way she wants, and you have no right to complain. You cannot spend a dime that belongs to her. It is natural that women think that men are there for their comfort. The man provides money for the well-being of his woman and his children, but with an educated ratchet, she has taken it to the extreme. She sees the dude as a thing that exists to ease her journey to the kind of lifestyle she deserves.

She expects that as a pretty one who has secured a job in an organization, she is hot stuff. She should get what she deserves from men. And those things she deserves include living a very comfortable life and having a smooth transition from singlehood to being married. She expects that any man who comes around her should want to marry her. She wants to dictate the pace in the relationship. She wants to decide when you stock up the house, when you go for shopping, when you entertain visitors, and when you hang around with friends.

She prefers you attend to her needs first before any other thing. If you are to choose between taking your sick mother to the hospital and taking this chick shopping, an educated ratchet wants you to take her shopping first.

Traditional type. If not for the shift in culture and social programming, this woman would be a dedicated wife and mother. In those days, a beautiful woman who went to college would easily find a good man with money to ask for her hand in marriage. She would marry this dude outright, have children for him, and lead a normal life. She would be dedicated to her husband because he would ensure that his family had everything they needed and take good care of the children. She would live her life trying to please her husband and her children. This is the kind of life that the educated ratchet would have led if it were one hundred years ago.

WHY IS THE EDUCATED RATCHET THE MOST DANGEROUS?

This chick is the most dangerous of all the types on the list. You have nothing to gain from dealing with this chick, but you have a lot to lose. You may lose your life if you are not careful. For the following reasons, you need to avoid this chick if you really love yourself.

1. She is so good at hiding her true identity.
2. She can surprise you at any time.
3. You are unsure of your place in her life.
4. She can kill you.

1. She is so good at hiding her true identity.

The educated ratchet has so many good features that look outstanding. On seeing her, you notice that part of her that depicts a clean profile, and you immediately fall in love with her, especially if you have had an encounter with any of the bad bitches. You would be amazed at how a lady with such class would be so well-mannered and industrious.

When you look closely, you notice the bad sides of these chicks. An educated ratchet has a tendency to be a ho. This chick can be a ho just like the thot, but she is better at hiding it. The thot will do it for everyone to know, but this chick won't do that. She is smart enough to do it and hide it somewhere safe. You would never believe that she has ever done anything of that nature.

When an educated ratchet ruins your life, you will never recover because she is going to hit you at that moment when you do not have the energy and zeal to make up for what she has scattered. She will disorganize you at an older age, when you have relaxed to enjoy what you have created out of life.

2. She can surprise you at any time.

No matter how long you have stayed with this chick, you can never brag that you know her because she can surprise you with a new act at any time. This chick can stay with you for years and have children for you until she wants to leave your side. Then she will come up with a story you cannot defend in the court. She'll leave with your children, half of your assets, and other valuable things, You are stuck in a crippled state. You find it difficult to recover from this because you didn't see it coming. You are relaxed because you had her to yourself, and then she struck. Within minutes, she took away from you what you spent the better part of your life building, and it may take you ten to twenty years to rebuild.

A lady had stayed with this dude for more than ten years. Anyone who knew this couple would never believe that they would one day have issues. I do not really know the bone of contention, One evening the cops came to lead the woman and her children out of the house. News later disseminated that the man was charged for assault and battery. The case went to court, and eventually the woman won. This guy nearly paid with his life for damages. The woman left with the children, his car, and the amount of money the court charged him to pay. The next time the chick came around was to pack her luggage.

These chicks know what they are doing. They have made their plans and pitched their tents. Whenever they know that they can make a lot of money, they strike. They play the long game, and they play for keeps.

3. You are unsure of your place in her life.

This chick would win the "greatest scam of the universe" award if there was something like that. You can be with this woman, but you won't know how she views you. This chick can be sleeping with the guy next door without your knowledge. She is so good at hiding things about her, and she can possibly have the guy next door as her walking dildo while you are the real guy, or vice versa. You do not really know your place in her life. You keep seeing the part of her that drew her to you without knowing that you are swimming in an ocean of uncertainty.

She has so many men in her life who perform different purposes. Some are there to buy her clothes, some buy her weaves, and others are simply playthings. You won't know the category you belong to in her life. You will introduce her to your friends as your woman, but she knows deep down that you are just her plaything. Flee from this woman before she uses you as a tool to achieve her selfish desires.

4. She can kill you.

This woman is so dangerous that if she is in a relationship with you, she can kill you and get away with it. This woman can get as far as spilling your blood. This knowledge has gone viral. People are aware of this, and they have incorporated it in TV shows to create awareness about this kind of woman. However, people seem to not get the information. This chick is so deadly that if killing you is the only way she can gain access to your resources, she will do it. She will arrange your death in such a way that no eye will ever suspect her. People would rather empathize with her, not knowing that she is the architect of the whole incident.

She can make your death look like a suicide, telling people that you have been acting weird. She may even say that she has been preventing you from committing suicide and that it was unfortunate that she was not around when you finally succeeded. She will cry while giving the statement to add more credibility to her story.

So many men have died in the hands of a kind of chick like this, but people do not know because they won't look at such a hardworking, pretty thing and imagine that she could ever soil her hands with blood.

I expect you to be scared of this type of woman by now. She is a woman who has all these aspects masked in a beautiful, ever-cheerful face.

CONCLUSION

Many men come to the hood to talk to women, but they do not know that there are so many types of women in the hood, and these different kinds of women have distinct features. Men are blindly moved by women's looks or first impressions, but they do not know how these women operate. They don't know that all the chicks in the hood do not have the same character. They may have encountered one of the good ones, and they are quick to judge that all the hood chicks are like that. Different women in the hood have different characters and different modes of operation. This does not deny the fact that some of them are good, but most of them are bad.

This book is an eye-opener, and the aim is to outline the five types of women you should try to identify the first time you meet them—and then run for your life. Some of these women are walking traps, and once you start talking to them, there is no going back. They will bring disaster to your life.

The major weapon you can fight these chicks with is knowing the way they operate. You can't fight what you do not know. You have to know and identify an enemy before you fight it, or else you may fight the wrong enemy. In the same vein, being able to point at someone and say, "This is a thot. That chick over there is a mammy," will help you avoid these chicks and reduce your chances of falling into the wrong hands.

These women are mean. When they are on your case, they make sure they get to the point where you cannot remember the road that will lead you home. When you are not strong enough to continue the race, then they desert you. They deal with you depending on how grievous your offense is or the level on which the chick operates. They may destroy your life to the level that you struggle to bring it back, or they can destroy it completely and leave you helpless—or dead.

It is important to note that you must not come to the hood to meet these chicks. You can meet them anywhere, especially the bad bitch and the educated ratchet, but they are products of the hood. You can meet them at expensive spots where dignitaries gather for an important function, and you think they are different from their counterparts in the hood. Where you meet them does not matter. What matters is that they still have the inherent gold-digging spirit. You can take a chick out of the hood, but you cannot take the hood out of the chick.

These chicks will eat you up without you knowing it. You only notice it when the deed has been concluded. She can be eating you and blowing on the injury, and you won't feel the pain. Run away from them. No matter how deadly and mean a dude is, he isn't as mean as these chicks.

You do not have to fall head over heels in love with a pretty chick. You may fall into the hands of a bad bitch or an educated ratchet, and you may not live to tell the story. She can be pretty and good, and you think she is not a bad bitch—but she can be an educated ratchet!

These five types of women that you need to avoid do not have uniform characteristics. Some are classy and some are not. Some are intelligent and others are not. That notwithstanding, these chicks will ruin your mind. Whenever you feel that you are with a woman with a similar character, run!

The thots will leave you complacent, and you will not attempt to find more in life. You cannot show that you are of a quality standard if you are dating a mammy. The hood rat can get you killed if you fuck with her. The bad bitch will drain your resources. The educated ratchet will ruin your life so that you can never recover. These women are out to get you. You need to do everything possible to stay away from these types of women.

Based on what you have to lose, you do not have to run from them—you need to fly from them. These chicks are so deadly and will suck the life out of you.

If the women you are dealing with display any of these attitudes, then it is time to find your way out of that relationship before it destroys you. Being in a relationship where you have no say is not worth it. A man is supposed to take his stance as the head of the household, making decisions where necessary and not giving up his position for a woman to take his place.

You need to take charge and be the real man in your marriage. You do not need to marry a woman who will take your place as the head of the family. Marrying a woman who has children out of wedlock will bring more harm than good to you. These women must have gotten involved with something bad out there.

Men should stop associating with single mothers. Almost all the chicks on my list can have children out of wedlock. You need to run away from them even if the women do not exhibit any of the traits mentioned.

Marrying or dating a single mother, especially when you do not have any kids yourself, can be disastrous. Even if she seems to be the perfect woman, it won't take long before she shows you her real character and several issues that you cannot handle. The following are probable situations that may arise while dating a single mother.

- They have been through tough situations and are used to fending for themselves. They have baggage, which has come as a result of their experiences in life. They have been abused, and it can cause them to be either of two extremes: they may become stronger women who have learned a lot from their ugly experiences, or they become weaker women who will easily give in to whatever life has to offer. Your presence in these women's lives will change nothing about them.

If you meet them at either of these dispositions, you will become a domestic medical practitioner, helping them to heal to your own detriment. For the woman who has become stronger, she has learned how to defend her children. She will value only her children and fight only for their interests, not considering how you feel about any decision she takes.

- You need to wear patience like a cloak. Things may not be moving as planned. You may decide to have a nice time with your wife, and the date will be canceled at the last minute because the babysitter canceled. If her children are older, they may find ways to get involved in unexpected behavior to prevent you from having access to their mother. To date a single mother is a load of work on its own.

You need to avoid having anything to do with these women because you may not have enough patience.

- The presence of the father is another threatening figure in the relationship. There is a strong possibility that the baby's father can come back at any time to become part of this woman's life again. Research has shown that men who have children with women always go back in the long run to reunite with the child and the baby mama. These women are likely to accept the fathers because of the bond they have shared. Most times, these women hold on to those relationships even without admitting it. They have strong hopes that the men will come back to them on a very good day. It is instinctual to want your children to have a good relationship with their father.

It is a known fact that women have special attachments to their ex. They find a way to defend them in a way that is uncomfortable to you. Being in a relationship with them is a waste of time. The ex can come back tomorrow, and the woman will give you tons of reasons why she should go back to him. She will leave your sorry ass to mourn.

- These single mothers will give you a condition that you should not discipline their children. As a matter of fact, most single mothers make it clear to you that you are not allowed to discipline their children until you have fully earned the respect of the children. Also, unlike a relationship where both of you learn how to discipline together, in this case you are not likely to have any influence over her methods. You may find it difficult to stomach the fact that a child is being disciplined in a manner that does not fall in line with your way of doing things.

Being in a relationship with this woman, and at worst case marrying this woman, spells doom for you. You have no say where her children are. You cannot discipline a child the way you deem fit because it goes against the mother's beliefs.

- The feeling is never the same. It will take a while for everyone involved—you, the woman, and her children—to accept and adopt this new family concept. Children often show resistance to seeing a new man in their mother's life when he proposes to be part of the family. They are often not comfortable when a man shows a certain degree of affection to their mother.

It may take years for the woman's children to see you as a father figure. It is very possible that they will never accept you as a father.

A man should get a woman who understands her position as a wife. She should be able to do the cleaning and cooking. You do not want the kind of wife who will turn the tables and make you the wife.

Men should find women who are submissive and understand the true position of the man, according to the man respect he deserves. You do not want the kind of woman who will preach feminism in your house and fight for equality.

A man can never be happy in a home where the woman is beautiful but will give him no peace of mind. Beauty is not the only thing dudes should consider in choosing their women. A woman can be facially beautiful but a devil at heart.

By now, you should be able to identify these toxic women and take appropriate precautions. If you are already dating one of them, run for your life before it's too late. A basket of joy follows a man who is disciplined enough to look beyond the surface view of these women and choose a woman who is not any of these five types.

Printed in the United States
By Bookmasters